THE FOREST OF DARTMOOR

The Reverend Henry Hugh Breton, M.A.

The
Forest of Dartmoor

By the Rev. H. HUGH BRETON, M.A.

FOREST PUBLISHING

First published 1931 (Part I), 1932 (Part II)
Republished in facsimile (combined edition) in 1990 by FOREST
PUBLISHING, Woodstock, Liverton, Newton Abbot, Devon TQ12 6JJ.

British Library Cataloguing in Publication Data
Breton, Henry Hugh b. 1873
   The Forest of Dartmoor.
   1.   Devon. Dartmoor, 1901–1936—Visitors' guides
   I.   Title
   914.23′5304823

ISBN 0-9515274-1-X

.

Forest Publishing

Sales and distribution by:
Town & Country Books
P.O. Box 31, Newton Abbot, Devon TQ12 5XH.

Editorial, design and colour photography by:
Mike and Roger Lang.

Typeset by:
Exe Valley Dataset Ltd, Exeter.

Printed and bound in Great Britain by:
BPCC Wheatons Ltd, Exeter.

CONTENTS

This single volume is a complete facsimile of the original two-part work and includes all of the illustrations and text from those works.

PUBLISHER'S NOTE

In presenting facsimile editions of these delightfully written little books by the late Reverend Henry Hugh Breton it is hoped that readers will not only find them enjoyable and interesting but also as an incentive to go out and explore Dartmoor for themselves.

The numerous contemporary photographs are particularly fascinating as now, in the present day, they combine to form an important pictorial record of parts of Dartmoor as they were in the early part of the twentieth century. Some also depict scenes that, sadly, no longer exist due to various changes that have occurred over the years, buildings and other structures that have long since vanished and a whole host of other aspects—even down to the type of clothes worn by our ancestors!

Bearing in mind that even the most recent of the books was written well over 50 years ago, there was a strong temptation to have the text revised, where necessary, so as to bring it up to date. However, after much consideration it was felt that to do so would spoil the whole context of the books, besides which they could no longer be strictly considered as being the work of the author. Instead, it was felt that the ideal solution would be for readers to carry out their own explorations and derive the additional pleasure (hopefully) of seeing the various changes that have occurred for themselves.

In undertaking any exploration of the Moor it must be emphasised that certain precautions need to be taken. In this respect your attention is drawn to Chapter III of The Beautiful Dartmoor Series—No. 1 which, although written such a long time ago, is largely just as relevant now as it was then. Because of extensive changes made over the years concerning the military use of Dartmoor, however, it is essential also to check that when visiting the northern Moor that the route does not encroach on any of the three military ranges—Okehampton, Willsworthy and Merrivale—when live firing is taking place. To assist in this respect details of the lists of firing dates and times are available for inspection at National Park Information Centres, local police stations, some Post Offices and certain hostelries on and around the Moor and are published once a week, usually on a Friday for the ensuing week, in some local newspapers. They can also be obtained by using the telephone answering service on the following numbers:

Torquay (0803) 294592   Exeter (0392) 70164
Plymouth (0752) 701924   Okehampton (0837) 2939

Finally, because no revisions whatsoever have been made to the text for the reasons stated, and in view of the various changes that have occurred in the intervening period since these books were first published, the publishers cannot accept any liability for any of the information contained within them.

FOREST PUBLISHING

INTRODUCTION TO
THE FACSIMILE EDITION

HENRY HUGH BRETON was born in Southampton on 16 September 1873 and was educated at Southampton Boys' College.

Shortly after leaving school he decided on ordination in the Church of England and was admitted as a Pensioner (the second of the three ranks in which students were matriculated) to Christ's College, Cambridge on 1 October 1892, prior to being formally admitted as a student in the University at Michaelmas, 1892.

In 1895 he obtained a Bachelor of Arts degree and entered Wells Theological College. Then, during the following year, he was ordained as a deacon—he was to be ordained as a priest (at Chichester) in 1897—and began his ministry as Curate of Christ Church, Blacklands, Hastings and was also Assistant Chaplain of Hastings Borough Cemetery. During his time here he obtained a Master of Arts degree (1899) and married his childhood sweetheart, Mabel Pennington Gorringe.

On 1 November 1907 he took up the living of Sheepstor, Devon which, in 1921, merged with Meavy to become Meavy with Sheepstor. He then exchanged for Alfriston, Sussex in the following year (1922) until vacating the benefice there on 1 August 1923.

Two months later, on 1 October 1923, he became incumbent at Morwenstow, Cornwall, an area previously renowned for smuggling and ship-wrecks. It was also an area immortalised by the Reverend Robert Stephen Hawker, a genuine eccentric, a natural wit and a poet and author. He had been vicar there from 1834 until his death in 1875 and amongst other great works of his was the origination, in 1843, of the Harvest Festival.

From there Hugh Breton moved to become incumbent at Dean Prior, Devon, on 21 May 1927, where, once again, he had a well-known predecessor. On this occasion it was the Devon Poet-vicar, Robert Herrick, who had been vicar of the Church from 1629 until 1674.

His last appointment was as Rector of Meshaw with Creacombe, Devon where he became incumbent on 29 May 1931 until vacating the benefice on 30 June 1933, when ill-health forced him to bring forward his retirement. He then moved to

Westham, Sussex (the home of both his and his wife's ancestors) where he lived until his death on 13 September 1936, and lies buried, with his wife, who died just over four years later, in the Churchyard of St Mary's Parish Church, Westham.

In addition to his pastoral duties, Hugh Breton was well known for his work with the Meteorological Office in London and during his life-time became a Fellow of the Royal Meteorological Society.

———————

Having spoken to a number of his former parishioners (to whom I should like to take this opportunity of expressing my sincere thanks), I can state with some authority that throughout his life Hugh Breton (and his wife) was both well-liked and highly respected. He also had a great sense of humour and one particular story that has been related to me illustrates this aspect only too well . . .

Whilst Vicar of Dean Prior he took great delight in telling his (amused) congregation during a Church Service about a certain prelate who, in the earlier years of his ministerial life, had asked a North Country farmer for an opinion as to how he was regarded by the Parishioners and been told "Well sir, we'll summer you and we'll winter you and then we'll tell you what we think of you".

Although I have received varying comments on the subject, it appears that he was at least partially deaf and had a slight speech impediment. One particular account concerning his speech, which was the source of some amusement to one of his former parishioners (a young lad at the time), was his inability to pronounce his "Rs" with the result that during Church services "Let us pray" would sound like "Let us pay"!

A quality of the man was his kind and good-hearted nature. He would give parties at the various vicarages for the Church choir and bell-ringers, was particularly sensitive to the needs of the children of the parishes in which he served (he had no children of his own), especially at Christmas time, and was always willing and prepared to take positive measures to raise money for charitable causes, one of which prompted him to write his first book . . .

———————

Even before taking up his appointment at Sheepstor it is quite apparent that Hugh Breton had already grown to love Dartmoor (see Chapter I of The Beautiful Dartmoor Series—No. 1). However, whereas previous excursions appear to have been mainly superficial he now began to explore the Moor in depth, kept copious notes and made a good number of friends with such notables as Robert Burnard, Richard Hansford Worth and Sabine Baring-Gould (the Squire and Rector of Lewtrenchard). Before long he also became an active member of the Dartmoor Preservation Association, playing an important role in the restoration of various ancient monuments and Dartmoor crosses, particularly within the Sheepstor parish.

As his knowledge of the Moor increased, and as a means of raising money towards a fund set up for the restoration of the Rood Screen at Sheepstor Church, he then embarked on his first book, which gave birth to "The Beautiful Dartmoor Series" (originally called "The Sheepstor Series") in 1911. In all, five volumes were published—two more on Dartmoor and another two on Cornwall—and so successful were they that all were subsequently reprinted, the first volume reaching its fourth edition. This, in turn, enabled some of the profits to be subsequently channelled into a new fund for re-seating Sheepstor Church with oak seats incorporating finely carved bench-ends.

Later, on becoming incumbent at Morwenstow, Hugh Breton returned to his writing activities and produced four more books under the collective name of "The Morwenstow Series of Shilling Books", the intention on this occasion being to direct the profits to the Church Restoration Fund. Whilst at Morwenstow he also raised money for the erection of a granite cross to Cornish design in memory of the mariners who lay buried there, besides holding two particularly memorable services (on 11 August 1924 and 5 August 1925) on the Atlantic shore at Duck Pool, which were called "Blessing the Sea". The reasons were three-fold:

1. "To invoke God's blessing on the sea, on the ships which navigate the sea, on the thousands of brave men who man the ships, both in the Royal Navy and in the mercantile marine".
2. "To pray for the fruits of the sea on which we are so dependent for our food supply".
3. "To remember before God those who have been drowned in the sea, especially those whose mortal remains have been washed ashore on the coast line of the parish of Morwenstow".

After vacating the benefice of Morwenstow, Hugh Breton went on to write no less than eight more books between 1928 and 1932, and once again devoted the profits to Church work, on this occasion part to an Improvements Fund of Meshaw Church and the other part to a fund for re-hanging the bells at Dean Prior. The titles included "Spiritual Lessons from Dartmoor Forest" (in two parts), "The Word Pictures of the Bible" (also in two parts), "The Great Blizzard of Christmas, 1927" and "The Great Winter of 1928–29". The final two were part of a projected series entitled "The Forest of Dartmoor" covering the South-east, South-west, North-east and North-west quarters of the Moor which, unfortunately, was never completed due to failing health. Furthermore, all attempts made to obtain any manuscripts, partially completed or otherwise, in connection with the second two parts of this series and also other projected titles prior to his death have failed. Instead, it appears that if there ever were any they have been destroyed.

MIKE LANG
January 1990

Part 1

South-East

The
Forest of Dartmoor

PART I.—SOUTH-EAST.

With some Ancient Records of Dartmoor Parishes and of Dartmoor Worthies.

From a Sketch by]   LEATHER TOR.   *[Mr. Charles Brittan.*

By the Rev. H. HUGH BRETON, M.A.

(Rector of Meshaw, near South Molton).

Author of "Beautiful Dartmoor," "The Breezy Cornish Moors," "Land's End and the Lizard," "The North Coast of Cornwall," "Morwenstow," "Hawker of Morwenstow," The Heart of Dartmoor," "The Word Pictures of the Bible," "The Great Blizzard of Christmas, 1927," "The Great Winter on Dartmoor, 1928-29," "Spiritual Lessons from Dartmoor Forest," "White Heather" and "Crystal Streams," &c,

PRICE 1/-   Postage 2d.

NEW DARTMOOR BOOK

by the Rev. H. HUGH BRETON, M.A.,

(RECTOR OF MESHAW).

"The Forest of Dartmoor"

PART I - - SOUTH-EAST

with Special Articles on " Some Ancient Records of Dartmoor Parishes," and on " Some Dartmoor Worthies," and
each part will also contain a Poet's Corner. Part I.
records a hitherto unknown poem of Robert Herrick's on
the " Parish Soldier," p. 52, and a simple confession of
his faith, p. 78.

Price 1/- Postage 2d.

from the Author or the Publishers.

The Books named below can still be procured from the Author.

Spiritual Lessons from Dartmoor Forest.

Part 1. **"White Heather"** and other studies.
Part 2. **"Crystal Streams"** and other studies.

All price 1/- each. Post 1½d.

The Heart of Dartmoor. Price 1/6 Post 2d.
(North-East and Centre).

The Dartmoor Snowstorm. Price 1/6 Post 2d.
(The Great Blizzard of Christmas, 1927).

A Great Winter on Dartmoor—(1928-29) with accounts
of the unprecedented snowstorm at Dean Prior of
February 16th, 1929, and the Great Ice Storm of the
closing days of February. Price 1/- Post 1½d.

ALL these books can be purchased from :
Rev. H. HUGH BRETON,
Meshaw Rectory,
South Molton, N. Devon]

The Forest of Dartmoor.

PART I—SOUTH-EAST.

▭

By the Rev. H. HUGH BRETON,

M.A.

(Rector of Meshaw, S. Molton).

▭

PRINTED & PUBLISHED BY
HOYTEN & COLE,
39, WHIMPLE STREET, PLYMOUTH.
1931.

BEDFORD HOTEL,

TAVISTOCK.

THE BEDFORD HOTEL, an imposing castellated Gothic building in the centre of the town, was erected about 1720 by Wriothesley, the third Duke of Bedford, for an occasional residence. It occupies a portion of the site of the Ancient Abbey, part of the refectory of which still remains, and which the Proprietor is pleased for his visitors to see. The Hotel is now replete with all modern requirements, for the comfort and convenience of visitors; including Hot and Cold water in every bedroom. Central heating. Officially appointed by the Royal Automobile Club, and the Automobile Association.

A charming adjunct is the delightful **Old Garden covering two acres.**

The extensive hotel yard is provided with excellent Garage accomodation. Posting in all its branches is done from here, and cars are let on hire.

Tavistock is by its geographical situation incomparably the most convenient centre in Devon and Cornwall for motoring and touring generally. Motorists making it their headquarters can visit any part of the two counties and return within the day, thereby avoiding the discomfort and waste of time in the packing which is involved in a continual change of habitation.

Salmon and Trout fishing, Golf (18 holes), Tennis, Croquet, Bowls, Hunting and Badminton in the winter.

UNDER PERSONAL SUPERVISION.

W. I. LAKE, Proprietor.

TO

HIS ROYAL HIGHNESS,

EDWARD, PRINCE OF WALES,

AND

DUKE OF CORNWALL,

THIS DESCRIPTION OF HIS FORFST OF DARTMOOR, DEVON.

Is humbly dedicated by the gracious permission of

𝕳𝖎𝖘 𝕽𝖔𝖞𝖆𝖑 𝕳𝖎𝖌𝖍𝖓𝖊𝖘𝖘 𝕻𝖗𝖎𝖓𝖈𝖊 𝕰𝖉𝖜𝖆𝖗𝖉,

MASTER FORESTER,

AND LORD WARDEN OF THE STANNARIES,

BY HIS LOYAL, FAITHFUL, AND MOST OBEDIENT SERVANT

H. HUGH BRETON.

Meshaw Rectory, Devon,
   July 1st, 1931.

JOSEPH GEACH & SONS,

Monumental Masons.

WORKS:

CEMETERY ROAD.

RESIDENCES:

14, DENSHAM TERRACE,

33, LANGSTONE ROAD, PEVERELL,

PLYMOUTH.

TELEPHONE 1016.

PREFACE.

I offer this little book to the public, the first part of a series of four on the great Forest of Dartmoor, hoping it will enable visitors and others to know more of this delightful playground.

All the profits will be devoted to Church Work, part to the Church Improvements Fund of Meshaw Church and the other part to the Fund for re-hanging the Bells at Dean Prior.

I thank these friends warmly :—

Mr. Charles Brittan, the Dartmoor artist, for the drawing for the Cover.

Mr. H. W. Harding for his pen and ink sketches.

Miss Gay, of South Brent and Mrs. Meade of Bull-hornestone, for their photos.

Mr. Hansford Worth for his sketch of the mortar stone.

Mrs. Fielden, of Torquay, for much information she has gleaned for me and for her poem.

Commander Morey, R.N., for the loan of his blocks.

H. HUGH BRETON.

Meshaw Rectory,
   South Molton,

July 1st, 1931.
For Contents see p. 72.

DEAN COURT.

Dean Prior.

CHAPTER I.

I. 1. **Dean Prior** is a small village on the main road from Exeter to Plymouth, 19 miles from the latter, and 21 miles from the former. Like many Devon and Cornish villages it has its Churchtown as distinct from its village. I will speak of the Churchtown first. It is one mile south of Dean Village, 3½ miles from South Brent, and 2 miles from Buckfastleigh. It consists of the vicarage, a farm, and a few cottages; in the midst is the parish Church.

THE CHURCH was rebuilt in the 15th century on a site of a Norman Church, of this older building only the font and a part of the tower remain. The present Church consists of chancel, nave, N. and S. aisles and tower. In the early Victorian period it was unfortunately stripped of everything of value and beauty by misguided 'restorers' It formerly had a Rood Screen and Parclose Screens, these were destroyed; also it had fine waggon roofs, these were also destroyed, all that remains are two scraps of the wall plates to be seen in the Church. Also it had ancient glazed tiles in the aisle floors, these, too, were destroyed, only two tiles now survive this "restoration," these are in the floor of the North aisle.

The recent restoration work was done in the incumbency of the Rev. C. J .Perry Keene, vicar for 48 years, to 1926. The new choir seats and the window in the S. aisle are to his memory, subject " The Presentation of our Lord." The E. window in the chancel is to the memory of the Devon Poet-vicar, Robert Herrick, vicar 1629 to 1674. The subject is " The Incarnation of our Lord."

The Font is a fine specimen of Norman workmanship, in the red Devon sandstone, there is a very similar one at Thurlestone.

The tower window is to the memory of the Rev. J. Buller Kitson, vicar for 33 years to 1866. The window at the W. end of the S. aisle is to the memory of the Parnell family.

INSCRIPTION ON DEAN BELLS.

1	JOHN YARDE, ESQ. 1 P 1734	....	diam.	30″
2	HAMBLINGS, BLACKAWTON, 1836	....	,,	31½″
3	W B I P.CH. WARDENS I PENNINGTON FECIT, 1734		,,	33¾″
4	I Y WILLIAM BRADRIDGE JOHN EDWARDS WDS HM IP 1734		,,	36″
5	JOHN YARDE, ESQ., WILLIAM BRADRIDGE JOHN EDWARDS, Wardens, 1734		,,	41″
	HARRY MUDGE (on the waist).			

The large mural monument in the S. aisle is to the
memory of Sir Edward Giles and his wife who were con-
temporaries of Herrick, whose verses are on the monument.   In the N. aisle the mural tablets are to the memory
of the Furze family who lived at Moreshead ; see my book
"Robert Furze, Gentleman."   There are also two slate
slabs let into the floor near the organ to the memory of
the same family, dates 1591 to 1609.   The mural tablet
on the vestry wall is to the memory of Herrick.

Photo by]   DEAN VILLAGE.   [*E. Tidey, Holne*

I. 2. **The Village** is a typical Devonshire village with very picturesque thatched cottages, especially at Higher Dean. It is now spoilt by a barbarous road widened for motorists. Dean Wood is a fine example of sylvan beauty; the Dean Burn brawles through the valley, and at two points forms fine waterfalls, the upper one is known as Hound Pool, where the old weaver of Dean Combe, whose spirit was turned into a hound, is condemned to expiate his sins by attempting the impossible task of emptying the Pool with a nutshell.

At the head of the valley is Cross Furzes on the N. side, and Lamb's Down on the West; a hunting path crosses the Dean Bourn below the former by a clapper bridge 11 ft. long; at the West end 1705 and G.R. are cut into the granite. This path crosses Skerraton Down and leads to Brent.

In Dean Combe, the Dean Bourn comes rushing down from the wild moors, forming more than one cascade. William Crossing, in his "Gems in a Granite Setting"† describes this valley with great charm of language. He says:—"The characteristics of this glen are truly expressed in its name. Here is the *Dene*, the leafy wood; the *burn*, the rippling stream; and each comes lovingly to the other. The brook hastens down from the bare heights to hide itself beneath the trees; the trees press forward to welcome it, and fling their veils of green over its silent pools and broken waters." In the Dean Bourn Valley the wild moor meets civilization. Doubtless a good deal of the land originally formed part of the moor, but has been reclaimed.

If the Dean Bourn is followed up 1 mile, a large portion of the old path has been washed away and a depth of several yards has been scooped out of this north bank of the river; this was done in the night of January 1st, 1928, during the great flood which accompanied the great thaw when the immense accumulations of snow which the blizzard deposited, went away in the night. (See "The Great Blizzard of Christmas, 1927," which may be obtained from the Author).

A little further on, at the point where the river bend rejoins the path, a tolmen will be seen in the river. The hole, which is not very large, shows that the river once ran at a higher level, and a pebble had become lodged in the boulder and by being swirled round an round, in the course of time had worn this hole.

Dean Prior formerly belonged to the Prior of Plympton. The little place was rendered famous in the seventeenth

Photo by]   DEAN BOURN.   [W. R. Gay, S. Brent

"Dean Bourn, farewell; I never look to see
Dean or thy warty incivility.
Thy rocky bottom, that doth tear thy streams
And makes them frantic, ev'n to all extremes."—*Herrick*

century by the poet Herrick, who held the living. Herrick, though he lived in a lovely country, disliked the uncultured tastes and uncouth manners of his parishioners. He was ejected from the living by the Puritans. in 1648, and from the joy he gave expression to on the occasion, it is evident that he hated his surroundings. Herrick was one of those people who somehow seem to fail to grasp that environment is one of the master-influences of the organic world, and one must adapt one's self to one's environment. Herrick lived to learn the lesson, and he admitted that his environment had in no small way contributed to the development of his poetic genius.

> " I must confess
> I ne'er have written such
> Ennobled numbers for the press
> Than where I loathed so much."

At the Restoration, Herrick was very glad to return to his living, and he died there in 1674, and was buried in the Chancel or in the Churchyard. From Dean Prior one can walk to Brent (3½ m.) One passes Marley House, formerly the seat of the Carew family, 2 m. from Dean village.

† Published by the *Western Morning News,* Plymouth.

* See the newly discovered poem of Herrick's, *p.* 52.

I. 3. WALKS FROM DEAN VICARAGE.

(i)   Up hill E. on reaching crossroads, and turn L. down to Dean Valley.

(ii)   Up hill E. passing the crossroads referred to above, and on to the direction post, then turn R. to Rattery Church.

(iii)   To Drybridge on main road, 1 mile S. of Dean Church. Before reaching the Bridge turn L. and go to Rattery Church.

Rattery Church is very beautiful, and has a magnificent Rood Screen restored in Memory of the late Misses Carew of Marley House. The Greenstone in the arcades is very beautiful. The Church has more than one good window. The pointed arch in the Tower is remarkably fine.

In the Churchyard near the S.E. corner of the Church is a flat slate slab bearing this inscription :—" Reader learn to die."

(iv)   Up hill W. to Fogen Plantation, here take the path left by the side of the plantation, this is a short length of the old Church path which led from Skerraton and the other farms to Dean Church.

On joining the road go L. up the little hill, then at the fork in the road keep straight on to Harbourne Ford ; the river is here spanned by a fine Clapper. Then ascend the hill, at the top turn R. and find your way through a gate on L. of the road on to Brent Hill.

(v)   At the fork in the road referred to in (iv. above) a stone on the grass marks someone's grave. Here turn R. past Golden Plantation $\frac{1}{4}$ m. beyond the lane which branches R. and leads to Moreshead House just below, by the stream.   (See " Robert Furze, Gentleman " which gives a description of this ancient Manor House now falling to pieces).

After visiting the old house, return to the point where the lane joins the road, then turn R. up the hill, this will lead on to Moor Gate, or turning L. just before reaching the Gate the road leads to Gigley Bridge ; the old ruined farm among the trees on R. is Reddicleave. (See Robert Furze Gentleman.") After crossing the bridge (the lane R. leads to Dockwell Farm), ascend the road to Easter Head ; from here a stray path leads W. on to Dockwell Ridge.   (IV. 6)

(vi)   To Fogen Plantation and on the second road, here turn R., then L., then almost immediately R. again into a narrow lane which leads down to Deancombe hamlet. Down this lane if you look over the first gate on L you will see a round stone built into the wall. This was only recently built into the wall, but stood inside the gate ; this is the lower stone of an old cheese press, which was formerly at Deancombe Farm ; it had a hook in the other side.

(vii)   Off main road take first turning to L. to Higher

Dean. On reaching the Cottage, turn L. and take the green lane which leads away from Higher Dean southwards. This is the old coachroad, London to Plymouth. (See "Spiritual Lessons from Dartmoor Forest, Part II. p. 13). This ancient road leads up to Fogen Plantation, on reaching it turn L. and return to Dean Church.

(viii) To **Deancombe.** Through Higher Dean, then turn L. and over Warm Bridge which spans the Dean Bourne. On crossing the Bridge turn L. and follow the road, which passes through Deancombe, and a very pretty road it is, with its brawling stream – the Dean Bourne beside the road. On R. before the stream leaves the road is the private path up into Dean Wood, where will be seen on L. a fine water-slide,– and further up on R. the Hound's Pool, a small but fine cascade.

The Dean Burn all along its course through the wood is very beautiful. About half-way up the wood a lateral stream comes down from the L. and joins the river. Above this is Skerraton Farm House, and near to the head of this stream are the ruins of an old Mill which flourished in 1300.

(ix.) To **Harbourneford and Brent.** To Fogen Plantation then turn L. and follow the road south to the Harbour River, here is the fine old clapper bridge which spans the river. To Brent keep straight on.

CHAPTER II.

HOLNE MOOR TO LID GATE NEAR HAYFORD.

II. 1. **Michelcombe,** Motor to Michelcombe, which is a pretty hamlet situated in a fold of the hills $\frac{1}{2}$ s.w. of Holne Village. It is a land of streams. The main stream is the Holy Brook.

> "Where He sendeth the springs into the rivers
> Which run among the hills."

The time to see Michelcombe is in the spring of the year, when the Orchards are pink and gay with the blossom of

the fruit trees.   Here is a Dartmoor Combe where the
apples thrive, and in the autumn the nuts and blackberries
The road north leads to Holne village.   The way on to
the Moor is to follow the lane past the farm and keep
straight on through the gate and up the green lane; in
less than a mile the moorgate is reached, and here we
enter upon Holne Ridge.   After crossing the Wheal
Emma Leat, and still following the footpath you enter
upon at the Moor Gate, in about $\frac{3}{4}$ m. five tumuli
will be seen in a row on R. orientated N.E.   From this
moor is a very extensive view, and on a warm summer's
afternoon it is a delightful spot to sit down and see and
think.

As you approach the N. side of Holne Ridge Paignton
Reservoir comes into view, and it is easy to return to the
road back to Holne by passing either on the E. or W. side.

The path from Michelmore on to the Moor is the old
SANDY WAY, a track which leads across the moor and
passes the East end of Fox Tor Mire and Whiteworks,
threading its way through the Mires and Aune Head a
mile after leaving the highest ground of Holne Ridge.

AT SCORRITON.

II. 2. **Scorriton.** On the Holne road from Buckfastleigh, $\frac{1}{2}$ m. after passing Hawson Court Gate four roads

meet. The one that turns sharp R. and leads down to the
Holy Brook, the next one R. to Holne; it is the road
straight on that leads to Scorriton, which is not a picturesque hamlet, but it has beauties around it. On getting
into the hamlet the road to L. leads on to Scorriton Down,
the track passes round the S. side of the Down, crosses
the Mardle river and in $\frac{1}{2}$ m. recrosses it. After recrossing
it, several hut circles will be seen, this track then runs
N.W. and joins the Sandy Way, which, as we have seen
comes up from Michelcombe.

On this track up from Scorriton, at the point where we
left the main track, a path turns R. up over Scorriton
Down, and running W., in $1\frac{1}{2}$ m. joins the last named
track at Hapstead Ford high up the stream, not far from
the Mardle Head, a little way beyond which it joins the
Sandy Way. If at the point where the former path crosses
the stream at the hut circles the stream is followed up to
its source, and the high ground climbed, you come on to
Snowdon Hill (see next note).

II. 3. **Lid Gate and Snowdon.** Motor from Dean or
Buckfastleigh over Wallaford Down - furzy waste ground,
and on past Cross Furzes — a heathery waste adjacent to
the woods of the Dean Burn, — and on past Hayford
House. Soon after passing this the road becomes a narrow
lane, follow this till you reach Lid Gate which opens out
on to the Moor. From this point are many fine excursions.
The car can be left inside the gate on the Moor, or on the
Waste on R. before the lane is entered.

II. 4. **Hayford Cross.** On entering on the Moor at Lid Gate
follow the track, and in $\frac{1}{2}$ m. the wall of Hayford Plantation
which you have had on your L. turns S; just before reaching the corner of the wall, between the track and the wall,
is an old Cross base, standing on its end in the miry
ground. It has this feature; the socket hole perforates
the stone,- a search near by in the wall might reward the
searcher with the find of the head, possibly built into the
wall.

The track we have been following from Lid Gate is the
one that leads to Huntingdon Warren House, which I
call Huntingdon Carriage Drive. Though rough in places
it is easy to follow, and passes over wild open country.

About $\frac{1}{3}$ m. after leaving behind the Hayford Plantation
wall, there is a fork in the path, and one path runs back
north-eastwards and leads down to Chalk Ford, where is
a foot-bridge across the Mardle river.

About 300 yards before reaching Chalk Ford four paths
meet, both those to L. run N.W. parallel to the Mardle
river, and in about 1 m. the path crosses the Mardle river
at HAPSTEAD FORD, $\frac{1}{3}$ m. beyond which the path joins the
Sandy Way. (II. 2.)

II. 5. **Huntingdon Warren House.** Follow the track
from Lid Gate, which is rather more than $1\frac{1}{2}$ miles from
the Gate.

The track from Lidgate is by far the easiest way to
reach Huntingdon Warren House. As one approaches
the House the ruin of Huntingdon Mine is passed on the
left hand, then cross the Wellsbrook and you are at the
Warren House. A house with its new take existed here in
the middle of the 16th century, but there is no mention of
it in the Survey of 1609. (For excursions from Huntingdon Warren House, (see Chap. III.)

II. 6. **Pupers Hill.** (1524 ft.) From Lid Gate (No. 3),
follow the Huntingdon Warren track about $\frac{2}{3}$ m., here
path forks. Take R. path and climb the gentle slope to
Pupers Hill,—this is Pupers Rock.

There are three piles of rock, on E. INNER PUPERS, and in
in middle, MIDDLE PUPERS, on which is a large group of
rocks called Pupers Rocks,—on W. OUTER PUPERS; the
ground sloping W. from the Rock down to the Wellsbrook
is strewn with boulders, the wash which disintegrated this
Tor evidently found a channel of escape by the Wellsbrook, which flows into the Avon, littering the hill-slope
with these errant blocks in its downward course.

II. 7. **Snowdon Hole,** (1522 ft.) After leaving Middle
Pupers above (leaving Outer Pupers on R.), steer N.W.
following the bond stones $\frac{1}{3}$ m. Here you come upon
Snowdon Hole which is an old miners' beam, a deep
hollow cut out by the old miners in Elizabethan times,—
(see my book "The Great Blizzard of Christmas, 1927,
also my reference to John Synge the Miner, in
my spring book of 1932,—"Robert Furze, Gentleman."

PETRE-ON-THE-MOUNT.

The hollow of Snowdon Hole continues S.W. down to the Wellsbrook, and this S.W. extension is Gibby Beam.

II. 8. **Snowdon Hill.** (1564 ft.) From the E. end of Snowdon Hole, steer almost due N. and in 300 yards you come upon the first of four Tumuli in a line S. and N., the circumferences of which are approximately 80, 50, 45 and 20 yards.

II. 9. **Ryder's Hill,** (1695 ft.) Also called Petre-on-the Mount. This is the highest point in this part of the moor, and naturally commands remarkable views of the Dartmoor Country, and also of the In-country.

On its crest is a bond stone known as PETRE'S BOUND STONE. To reach Ryder's Hill from the northern-most tumulus on Snowdon Hill (see II.8), steer North $\frac{1}{3}$ m then turn W.N.W. for about $\frac{1}{2}$ m. to avoid the swamp at head of Wellsbrook Girt, and climb to the Summit of Ryder's Hill.

It may also be reached from Hapstead Ford, steering W.S.W. It is rather less than 1 m. from there (I. 3. ii.) also see II. 1. Keep away from this very high land in foggy weather, as it is very frequently covered with dense cloud fog.

HUNTINGDON WARREN.

CHAPTER III.—HUNTINGDON WARREN.

From this point there are several delightful excursions, but the ground is wild and rough, and one must be prepared for some rough walking.

III, 1, **To Ryder's Hill.** From the Warren House cross the Wellsbrook by the Clapper, and steer N. parallel to the Wellsbrook Marsh, (keeping it on your L.) Continue in this direction, keeping on the hard ground until *the head* of the Wellsbrook Girt is reached, here is a Bond Stone, and from this stone steer N.W. and in $\frac{1}{2}$ m. you ascend the hill. (II. 9.)

III. 2. **To Lidgate and Hayford, Buckfastleigh** : — Cross the Wellsbrook and follow the Huntingdon Warren House carriage drive (II. 3,).

III. 3. **To Brockhill Ford.** Cross Wellsbrook and steer S.E. over the highest ground of Hickaton Hill, where you will find a good pound enclosing hut circles. Continuing S.E. you will come upon the Brookhill Ford which gives safe passage across the Brockhill Mire, which runs nearly two miles. Before approaching the Ford, notice the several pounds enclosing hut circles on the W, side.

The Ford was crossed by the Abbot's Way, which passes Water Oak Corner Plantation. Now after re-crossing the Ford, turn West and follow the Abbots' Way to Huntingdon Cross, and from there back to the Warren House, noticing Biller's Pound with a group of Hut Circles outside its western boundary. This Pound is on R. just before descending to the Old Cross.

III. 4. **To Huntingdon Cross.** Follow the Wellsbrook down to where it joins the Avon. This ancient Cross marks the boundary of the Duchy lands, which at this point join the lands of Lord Churston. It was standing in 1557, and is probably 300 years older than that. It is $4\frac{1}{2}$ ft. high. (See p. 33).

The Cross marks a ford across the Avon, which the Abbot's Way crosses here. At the Cross the parishes of Dean Prior, Brent, Harford, and Princetown meet.

The large cairn on the hill W. of the Warren House is called "**Heap o' Sinners.**"

Huntingdon Clapper.

ON AVON nr. HUNTINGDON CROSS.

III. 5. **To Huntingdon Clapper and Huntingdon Stone Circle.** From the Warren House pass down along the west bank of the Wellsbrook, and as you approach the Avon turn R. and follow the river up until it bends. At the bend the river which comes down from the N. turns and flows E. past the Wellsbrook Valley.

The Clapper Bridge is a structure with two openings and spans the Avon at a picturesque place. One stone is in the river, dislodged from its position by a heavy flood.

One can cross the river at this point by jumping from the end of the remaining stone; if you stand on this stone looking S. you will see standing stones peering above the brow of the hill 150 yards from the Bridge.

The Circle is double, except at its high end on W. It has been the containing circle of a cairn or tumulus. At the higher end the tumulus did not need much support, at the lower end it did, and in consequence the Circle is doubled there with good sized stones. One of these stones is a white spar stone.

(See Spiritual Lessons from Dartmoor Forest, part 2, page 20.)

III. 6. **Western Whittabarrow** (1575 ft.) From the Circle one may continue southwards and climb to Western Whittabarrow, near whose south side are the remains of Petre's Cross.

Skerraton Longstone.

Photo by]   SKERRATON LONGSTONE.   *[Capt. Stone*

III. 7. **Eastern Whittabarrow** (1539 ft.) This huge cairn may be reached by steering east from Western Whitta-barrow from which it is only ¾ m. distant. This is the finest cairn in this part of Dartmoor, and is a very con-spicuous object for miles around.

From the cairn descend N. direction to the Avon at Huntingdon Ford which may be crossed, and from this point it is an easy stroll up the Wellsbrook Combe, back to the Warren House.

CHAPTER IV.

From SKERRATON GATE.

IV. 1. **Skerraton Farm House** stands on the site of an ancient Manor House. Much information about the ancient Manor of Skerraton will be found in my book—"Robert Furze, Gentleman." The name has several variants "Sciredun," "Shiridon, (1502)" "Skyridon," once held on condition that the owner provided two arrows for the King when he hunted on Dartmoor.

It is named in the Domesday Book, and in 1275 was owned by John Boyvile, who had married the daughter of the then owner, Walter Medicas. Like many other lands in England it became the possession of Henry VIII, who sold it to Basset, who sold it to Robert Furze of Mores-head. Furze built many of the newtake walls enclosing moorland on the west side of the house. These dilapidated walls or rather banks may still be seen.

IV. 2. **Skerraton Longstone.** Passing on to the open moor through Skerraton Gate a few hundred yards N.W. is this fine longstone, which is a conspicuous object on Skerraton Down, and is situated only a few yards from the source of the Harbourne River. This fine stone leans towards S.and is 8½ ft high.

IV. 3. **Parnell's Hill** is the hill West of the Longstone; On the hill are two Cairns, 90 ft. and 75 ft. respectively in diameter. From the Cairns turn N. and strike the cart track to Huntingdon Warren, and go out to the Warren House. (II. 5).

IV. 4. (i) **Skerraton Gate to Cross Furzes** (a favourite meeting place of the Dartmoor Hounds). Follow the wall which runs N.W. from the Gate, keeping it on one's right hand; at $\frac{1}{2}$ m. pass through the Gate and on past Lambs' Down Farm ruins, and follow the path down the hill to the Ford. Ascend the hill, and on gaining the road above is Cross Furzes, where several roads meet.

At the Ford a footbridge spans the Dean Prior. The bridge is a single clapper, nearly 12 ft. long. At the W. end is the date 1705, and letters G.R., and about the middle of it this inscription, — " B.D.A. 1737."

At this Ford the Abbot's Way crosses the Dean Bourn. Here we can return to the open Moor by this ancient way which crosses Lambs' Down, at the top of which it crosses the leat, and goes on to Water Oak Corner Plantation. At this point it may be followed W. across the moor, and in less than $\frac{3}{4}$ m. it crosses the Brockhill Mire at Brockhill Ford (II. 3), or at Water Oak Corner turn sharp L. and follow the wall back to Skerraton Gate. and as one nears Skerraton Gate the way is along a wide green track, with grass of very fine texture a feature of some of the moorland paths.

IV. 4, (ii.) **To Cross Furzes Clapper and Lambs Down** Farm (1,050 ft.). The easiest way to reach these places is to motor to Cross Furzes, and from there follow the wall that runs S. down to the Dean Bourn; this wall forms the W. boundary of the waste land, and leads you right down to the bridge. Or, if the grass is wet, take the path from Cross Furzes which runs S.E. across the waste ground, and when it reaches a wall turn S.W., this path leads to the bridge. From the bridge ascend the opposite hill by the cart track which runs up the hill in a S.E. direction; it passes by the ruined walls of the Farm and the clump of beech trees on the E. side of the Farm ruins, which were planted there to protect the Farm from the fierce mountain winds. If the path is followed it leads to a hunting gate which opens on to the moor. (See IV. 4., i.) The hearth stone at Lambs Down Farm survives and it is a cracked millstone.

IV. 5. (i). From **Dean Church Gate** motor to MOOR CROSS (I. 3. 5) then walk up the Green Lane, which runs N. till you reach Dean Gate which opens on to the Moor. Look ing N. Skerraton Longstone is seen on the rising ground E. of the Harbourne Valley. It is an easy walk on the spongy turf to it.

(ii). Turn L. from the gate along wall, cross the river and steer W., keeping along the base of Parnell's Hill as you approach the Avon Valley. The line of bond stones on your left hand, which run from Dockwell Hole right on to the Avon, have a conspicuous Longstone 5 ft. high at the point where it crosses the north end of Dockwell Ridge, which I think is a genuine longstone which may have formed a Circle at this spot. As you approach the river turn R. over Smallacombe plains, and follow the river up. Soon the Brockhill stream is crossed just before it joins the Avon. Just beyond this, running up from the river is a row of standing stones named the THREE BROTHERS. These are thought to be a stone row, but they are probably the stones of an old newtake wall. A little further along, near the stream are the ruins of a Blowing House. It is a pleasant walk up the valley, keeping away from the stream, up to Huntingdon Cross, and thence on to Huntingdon Clapper and on to Clayworks Bridge. A little way after passing Huntingdon Clapper are the remains of a hut on R. which the tenant of Huntingdon Warren many years ago used as a Watch-house to catch poachers—men who were at that time working in the Naptha Works. (See also V. 4.)

IV. 6. To the **Dockwell Gate,** motor either from Dean Churchtown past Fogen and Golden Plantations, continuing up the hill, and just before reaching Moor Gate turn L. and over Gigley Bridge, and onward to Easter Head (951 ft.) From the waste ground here is a wonderful view; the Moor W. and N., and the sea and Dartmouth, East and South.

From Easter Head go down the wide stray which leads west to the Moor. (I. 3, v.) Dockwell Gate is soon reached. From the Gate are these fine walks : —

(1) Follow the wall on L. to Shipley Tor, from which is a very fine view of the Avon Valley.

(ii) From the Gate follow the green trackway (which

Harbourneford Clapper Bridge

leads over to Parnell's Hill, and on from there to Combe-
stone Tor near Hexworthy), and on reaching the southern
slopes of Parnell's Hill ascend the hill and see the Cairns
(IV. 3), and then turn E. to the Longstone, and thence
back to Dean Gate. and back by the green lane and Moor
Gate, (IV. 5, ii.)
(iii) Follow the track till the Menhir at the N. end of
Dockwell Ridge is reached, then continue as iii. 5 (ii).

CHAPTER V.

SOUTH BRENT.

V. 1. **South Brent Church** shared the same fate of
spoilation suffered by so many Devonshire Churches in
the nineteenth century. It retains very little of interest
to the lover of beautiful churches except the Norman font,
which is beautifully carved, and also the ancient belfry
door. The original church was Norman, and small portions
of the original structure still remain. Brent formerly
possessed an octagonal cross, but it was wantonly destroyed
by a builder many years ago. There are also well carved
new oak choir stalls and organ case given by the
Cholmondely family. Portions of the old Rood Screen
were found in 1924 and sawn up and converted into Altar
Rails – an unfortunate error of judgment.

V. 2. On to **Brent Hill** (1017 ft.) for extensive views.
(i) A footpath opposite Whinfield leads to the Beara
Common, which is part of the hill.
(ii) Motor to Higher Lutton, here turn up the lane R.
which brings you out under the rocks on the west side of
the hill.
(iii) Motor through Lutton. $\frac{3}{4}$ m. beyond turn R. up a
lane, this leads to the north end of the hill.

V. 3. To **Shipley Bridge** which is a charming spot.
(i) Beyond the lane noted above, turn L. by Downstow,
$\frac{1}{4}$ m. further on. At Yalland Cross turn L. and the road
soon descends to the Bridge.
(ii) Motor via Lydia Bridge and Aish, and there keep

straight on up the Valley; in 2 m. the Bridge is reached.
$\frac{1}{3}$ m. before reaching the Bridge, Diamond Lane turns up
the hill on L., this track leads up to the Moor past Ball
Gate, outside which is the Coringdon Cromlech (V.I. 4,
IX). The wall on L. from here may be followed on to
Glasscombe Corner (V.I. 4, XI).

V. 4. From Shipley Bridge ascend the hill on L. behind
Clay Works, and keep up to **Black Tor.** On the way you
pass two Pounds which are smothered in fern in summer.

SHIPLEY FALLS, SOUTH BRENT.

Leaving the Tor on R. steer N., keeping up to avoid the
rough ground. Soon you come to **"The Rings"** which in
1930 were investigated by the Dartmoor Preservation
Society, and photos taken and records made by Mr. R. H.
Worth.

From the Rings N.W. $\frac{1}{4}$ of a mile you come to a footpath.
Follow this down to the river, and cross there. On the
Moor, east of the Brockhill Mire, is a long row of stones

in a line with what looks like the slight remains of a stone row with a circle at its western end. (IV. 5., ii.)

After leaving the Brockhill Brook strike the Abbot's Way just above, and follow it to Huntingdon Cross.

On **Hickadon Hill** which we pass before reaching the Cross, is a perfect Pound with Hut Circles.

From The Cross follow the Avon up. On the slope of the hill are good Pounds. Further on at the point where the Avon turns N. is an old pack-horse bridge with huge blocks. One is in the river. (III. 4.)

Standing on this bridge looking South, about 150 yards away on the skyline are the stones of Huntingdon Circle, (III. 5.)

V. 5. On the way to the Shipley Waterfalls which are 100 yards above the bridge, on the L. of the path is a large boulder, with the Initials of once famous huntsmen, men who for many years hunted with the Dartmoor Hounds.

6. Return to the Bridge, cross it, and at Shipley Cottage on L. a path climbs up the hill side on E. side of the river to **Shipley Tor**. This path may be continued on to the Moor, or turn E. and follow the wall E. (IV. 6. i,)

7. Ascend the Bala Brook. Keep on the North side of the river and follow it up. At the head of the valley on the same side is an isolated building—Father Abe's House, which formerly served as a stable for the horses employed at the Clay Works.

CHAPTER VI.

From Wrangaton Station Crossroads.

The Avon Watershed.

VI. 1. To **Owley Gate** either by car to Owley Farm (or by bus to Wrangaton Cross Roads, then turn R. and pass the Cheston Farms, then on to Owley Farm). The Mill below is no longer worked, but the old mill stones are there. Then turn from the Farm L. along the narrow lane which leads to Owley Gate, which opens on to the open Moor.

VI 2. Here are three paths :- Take the RIGHT first, and go down towards the river, and after crossing the Scad

Brook and another small streamlet, keep near the river and follow the path through the trees till you come to the **Wishing Pool** (p. 68). This is quite a fine Gorge, like Lydford Gorge on a small scale. 50 yards N.W. of the Wishing Pool is a ruined **Blowing House** with its old wheel pit. Just as you approach the ruin there lies a triangular stone, with its base resting on the ground (see p. 69). On two sides of the triangle are two mortar stones. I have never seen one quite like it. In wet weather, to avoid swampy ground, keep above the Scad brook and the streamlet beyond, then descend to the gorge. (See p. 71).

VI. 3. Retracing one's steps as one reaches the Scad Brook at the point where the Scad Brook flows into the Glazebrook is a ford which leads to Corringdon Farm. Recently a fine well-shaped bronze axe-head has been found near, and is now in possession of the finder at the Farm. Return to Owley Gate.

VI. 4. Take the LEFT path, which leads to Harford, when on reaching Spurrell's Cross you come to a group of remains :

(i) *Spurrell's Cross.* The head is crocketed. Recently re-erected by the Dartmoor Preservation Association. A good piece of work.

(ii) *Barrow* about 100 yards S.W. of the Cross. Two stones of a ruined containing Circle. Double stone-row running N. for 140 yards.

(iii) A short distance S a large Cairn—no circle, no row.

(iv) 150 yards East, another Cairn with 4 raised Cairns at the corners. One destroyed.

(v) Then turn N. and go to the top of Glasscombe Ball. Another large Cairn crowns it.

(vi) Steer down the hill N.E. for *Glasscombe Corner,* and you soon come upon another *stone row* with moderate sized stones running almost direct to Glasscombe Corner. It is about 140 yards long.

(vii) On reaching Glasscombe Corner follow the wall, and in ¼ m. you reach the East Glazebrook. Just before crossing the stream is a low tumulus, from which runs S. an Avenue with 8 or 13 parallel rows.

(viii) After crossing the E.G. you come upon another Avenue with 4 rows, which leads up to a semi-circle.

HUNTINGDON CROSS.

(xi) Still follow the wall to Coryndon Ball Gate. Here on a low long mound is **Coryndon Cromlech.** Here is a genuine Long Barrow, with the ruins of a Cromlech at its eastern end. Ruined Capstone is 11 ft. 6 in. x 8 ft., height of supports, 6 ft. Barrow is 55 ft. long. From here follow the wall till you come to Diamond Lane, through which descend to join the main road to Shipley Bridge. (V. 3, ii.)

VI. 5. At Wrangaton Station Cross Roads (vi. 1.), turn up Green Lane, the road to the Golf Links. In ¾ m. Wrangaton Gate, which opens on to the Moor, is reached. (i) From here ascend the hill and explore Eastern Beacon. and the rocks of Ugborough Beacon. There are two Tumuli in the former, and one on the latter.

VI. 6. Follow the path from Wrangaton Gate over the Golf Links, across the southern slope of Eastern Beacon, which leads on in less than 1 m. to the Spurrell's Cross, and the group of remains around it. (vi. 4).

CHAPTER VII.

BITTAFORD AND CANTRELL.

VII. 1. Take the road past the Asylum. Soon after turn L., and this will bring you to the Golf Links.

VII. 2. Turn *under* the Railway Arch on W. side of the Brook. The lane leads up past West Peek House, and on to the open Moor. Here is Cuckoo Hall. On L is a path which leads up the hill to Butterdon Hill.

VII. 3. Return to the main road, and go on towards Plymouth till the Clay sheds with the tall chimney are reached. Here turn up under the railway, and follow the lane which leads up to Cantrell Gate which opens on to the Moor. Above is the terminal point of the Clay Works line to Redlake Clay Works.

Strike the line and follow it W. till you reach a quarry, here is a double stone row, **Cantrell Stone Row**.

VII 4. Return to the Plymouth road and go a little way towards Plymouth, and at the point where the corners have been rounded off in widening the road, turn up *over*

Block lent by]

HARFORD BRIDGE.

[Commander Morey, R.N.

the Railway. Soon a gate opening on the Moor is reached, with beech trees on the R.; from this gate ascend straight up to **Western Beacon**   ....
or from the Gate turn L. keeping above the Wall. Soon you are at Lukesland Quarry. From here a path leads N. along the wall, passing Addicombe. Then continue to follow the path which still runs parallel to the wall, and ın ½ m. you reach Tor Rocks. Just before reaching them you can turn L. down a lane which leads to Broomhill Farm, on the road Ivybridge to Harford, or instead of taking this lane you can keep straight along the path from Addicombe, and on leaving Tor Rocks well on L. continue till you come to Harford Moor Gate, where you can turn L. down the lane, and see Harford Church, VIII. 2.

VII 5. **Western Beacon** (1088 ft - see above), has a semi-circle of tumuli on the top. From one of them a stone row runs N. and passing through Black Pool terminates in a longstone on the rising ground of Butterdon Hill.

VII 6 From the Longstone ascend Butterdon Hill, (1204 ft.) Here are more large Cairns. Just beyond them from a small circle a stone row runs a considerable distance N., in ½ m. from the Circle passing Hangershell Rock which stands on the left hand. ½ m. further on the track-way we cross runs from Owley Gate (VI. 4.) past Spurrell's Cross (VI., 4., i.), and on to Harford Moor Gate. Along this path prisoners of war and travelling sailors used to pass on their way from Plymouth to Exeter, although most of them came through Dean Prior.

CHAPTER VIII.

IVYBRIDGE.

1....*Village.*   2....*Harford Bridge.*   3....*Erme Valley.*

VIII. 1. **Ivybridge** is on the fringe of Dartmoor. It is in very close touch with some of the finest river scenery on the moor. The village is built on the banks of the Erme, and is at the mouth of the delightful gorge through which the Erme comes brawling down from the moors.

Several days may be very well spent in thoroughly exploring this part of the moor. The high ground lacks the ruggedness of the Northern Quarter and the Western borders of the moor, but all real lovers of the moor will appreciate its beauties. The easiest way to see this interesting country is to make the four railway stations — South Brent, Wrangaton, Ivybridge and Cornwood — starting points for excursions, ascending one river, crossing the ridge, and down the river in the next valley.

Hanger Down. Ascend the W. bank of the Erme under the railway arch; 1 m. after passing through Pill Hill Farm, a lane will bring you out on to the slopes of Hanger Down. Cross the down to the clump of trees, then follow the track running N., and on coming out on the road turn R. and continue to Harford Bridge The Erme at Harford Bridge is very pretty, both up and down stream.

VIII. 2. Motor to **Harford Church,** (2 m.) a typical Moorland Church with much good new oak in it, otherwise is very bare, having been stripped of all its beauty many years ago. There is a very ancient tombstone in the churchyard on the N. side of the Church, and an old altar tombstone. From the road round the Church are fine views of the Erme Valley and Tristis Rock.

VIII. 3. **Tristis Rock.** At Harford Bridge on its W. side a path winds up the Moor to this fine rock, from which a grand view of the Erme is obtained, and near the rock on its south side are two stone rows (see p. 38).

VIII. 4. **Harford Moor.** On S. side of the Churchyard, a road leads E. to Harford Moor Gate which opens on to the Moor. (VI. 4, VII 4). At the N. end of Harford Moor is a fine example of the Kistvaen, but it has lost its capstone.

VIII. 5. **Pile's Wood.** Continuing N. from the Kistvaen, this ancient wood will be seen above the east bank of the Erme, and extends nearly $\frac{1}{3}$ m. with its dwarfed trees like Wistmans' Wood. Its altitude (1,000 ft.) is not nearly as great as Wistman's Wood, hence the trees are not so stunted in their growth. Not far from its N. end is a pile of rocks called the Dungeon, the place of sanctuary of many a hunted fox. I add a letter of mine to "The Western Morning News" on this subject. About $\frac{1}{2}$ mile

TRISTIS ROCK, HARFORD.

N.E. of the wood is THREE BARROWS HILL (1522 ft.) $\frac{1}{2}$ m.
N.N.W. of which are the remains of Hobajohn Cross.
Return to Harford Church.

TREES ON DARTMOOR.

Sir,—A correspondent recently said that trees only grew
on the higher parts of Dartmoor, at Wistman's Wood. I
could shew him several places where they grow, or have
grown in past ages.

There are considerable collections growing now at Piles
Wood, on the Erme, and at Black Tor Copse, on the West
Oakment. Bog oak has been dug up in the peat tyes on the
high ground near Broad Rock, just above the head of the
Erme. I found the remains of what must have been a huge
spreading oak tree at the foot of Buttern Hill, 1300 ft. above
sea level. In the marshes and peat tyes on the Walla Brook,
(on the N. Teign) below Western Tor, considerable quantities
of oak have been brought to the surface and burnt in the
moormen's fires. This ground is 1400 ft. above sea level.

William Crossing, in his " Guide to Dartmoor," mentions
that a place called by moorsmen as " Fur Tor Wood,"
(pp. 176, 481), and also in his " Gems in a Granite Setting"
(pp. 27 to 30), near Fur Tor, at Cut Combe, remains of trees
have been found. This ground is about 1,700 ft. above
sea level. Trees never grew all over Dartmoor, but there is
conclusive evidence that there was considerable growth of
timber in the sheltered combes at great altitudes, which
proves that the Dartmoor climate at one time must have
been much more genial than it is now. These large trees
could not possibly grow there now.

H. HUGH BRETON,

Dean Prior Vicarage, Buckfastleigh.

April, 10th, 1928.

VIII. 6. The lane N. of the Church leads to Bullaven
Farm, the home of Comdr. Morey, R.N., who receives
guests in his charming moorland retreat, with so many
facilities which contribute to the enjoyment of a moorland
holiday. Fishing in the great stretch of the beautiful Erme
and hunting and shooting on the Moor, and the invigorating Dartmoor air, and the charming scenery all round.

VIII 7. From **Pile's Wood** follow the Erme up nearly a
mile. On L. a small stream running through a shallow

Block kindly lent by]

THE RIVER ERME—see VII., 6.

[Commander Morey, R.N.

Photo by] PILES WOOD. *[W. R. Gay*

combe joins the Erme. Near the banks of this stream is
the Beehive Hut.

Still another mile further up the Erme you come to Erme
Plains. A little way above on the W. side of the river is
a stone circle, from which the LONG STONE ROW starts
and runs over hill and dale up to Green Hill, where it
terminates in a Barrow – a distance of 2½ miles.

VIII. 8. On the east side of the river above Erme Plains,
is **Brown Heath** Where the Hook Lake joins the Erme
there are the remains of a Blowing House.

A little further on, on the east side of the Erme is a
Pound. From this a stone runs N. and terminates in a
Stone Circle enclosing a Kistvaen. ½ m. further N., Red
Lake is reached, and just above are the Red Lake Clay
Works situated in almost impassable swamps. From here
the mineral train starts and journeys to Cantrell, near
Bittaford (VII. 3) puffing, snorting, screeching and
shrieking on its way to drive cattle off the line. It is not
furnished with a cow-catcher, hence so much noise as it
bears its white truck loads down to the drying sheds at
Cantrell, on the Ivybridge – Plymouth road.

CHAPTER IX.

CORNWOOD.

1....The Village.   2....Stall Moor.   3....Cho'wick Circle and Stone Row.   4....China Clay Works.   5....River Yealm.

IX. 1. **Cornwood** has a picturesque village, which is situated on the southern borders of Dartmoor. It is an excellent centre for exploring the Yealm and the many delightful nooks which that river affords. The parish Church is perpendicular, with an early English chancel. Within is a small monument to the memory of Robert Bellmaine and his wife, which begins very appropriately with the inscription, "Here's rest and peace."

IX. 2. **Stall Moor.** There is a very fine stone row on this moor above Cornwood. The stones are unusually large for those of a Dartmoor stone row. The row is single and consists of 68 stones, and it is 1640 ft. in length.

XI. 3. **The Yealm** should be explored from its mouth to its source. The pleasantest way to visit it is to take the steamer from Plymouth, a trip of only 6 m. On the way the Mewstone is passed, a precipitous rock detached from the mainland. The mouth of the Yealm and its tidal waters are extremely beautiful. Upon the banks stand the villages of Newton Ferrers and Noss Mayo. In places the woods fringe the water. The sheltered harbour affords secure anchorage for yachts of all sizes.

XI. 4. **Hawns and Dendles** is a very pretty wooded valley on the Yealm, N. of Cornwood, but it is too well-known to need description. The river rolls through the wood over its rocky bed, and forms pretty cascades.

The Yealm rises in the bogs above Shavercombe Head. The way to reach Hawns and Dendles is motor to Combe near Wisdom Mill. From here take the path which runs along by the river, which can be followed up a long way. On leaving the wood quite 1 mile N. of the Mill there is a foot bridge across the river. At this point you can enter upon the open moor. Here you can ascend the river to the Blowing House.

XI. 5. A little above the **Blowing house,** which is a fine example of the old tinners' Smelting-house with its mould stones, is the Yealm Steps, small but pretty cascades tumbling down over the boulders, well worth a visit after a heavy rain. It is a wild and pretty spot.

XI. 6. From Wisdom Mill follow the lane up to and past North Hele Farm. From this point it runs N. and in $\frac{1}{2}$ m. the river is crossed, just before it is joined by Broadall Lake Here are two paths, the one L. follows up the Broadall Lake Stream, the one R. soon leaves the wood and you find yourself on the open moor.

XI. 7. **Dendle's Waste Stone Circle** is situated close to the east side of the wall which runs S. to N. across the highest part of Dendle's Waste. It contains 9 stones and has a diameter of 10 ft., and encloses a Kistvaen which has been rifled.

$\frac{1}{4}$ m. N.W. where the Broadall Lake bends, a little way above of the west side of the stream, are several Pounds with hut circles. If the wall referred to above which passes the circle is followed up, you come to a gate where you enter on the moor. In dry weather you can steer N. over the hill with its bogs, and down the other side into the Langcombe Valley.

Ancient Records of Dartmoor Parishes.

1.—DEAN PRIOR.

THE CONSTABLES' ACCOUNTS.
Section I.   1567 to 1600.

Photo by   DEAN PRIOR CHURCH AND CHURCHYARD.   *E. Tidey, Holne*

From the Pink Book of Dean Prior.

These accounts at Dean were during this period worked by the iiij men, and most carefully and fully done.

Who were the iiij men?—At Dean—"The Masters of the Parish."   Even the Churchwardens exercised their office in many ways "by Command of the iiij men."   It is quite a mistake to assume that these most important officials of a parish were an arbitrary oligarchy; they were no more an oligarchy in the modern sense of the term than the Churchwardens or the Parochial Church Council is an oligarchy; neither were they appointed for life. It is true that the supreme power was vested in the hands of a few, but they were duly appointed by the parish, and for one year at Dean, but they were re-appointed the second year and then dropped out. In the second year the two newly-appointed in the previous year became the seniors. They were usually the principal men in the parish, but the indispensable qualification was that they should be "*good and honest men*."

At Dean in the stress which preceded the Armada there were the viij men for three years in succession, but it reverted to iiij men in the Armada year.

During this period the incomparably greatest of the iiij men was Robert Furze, of Moreshead, who was the shining example of the parish in unsparing and strenuous service for more than forty years – a really great man who ought never have been forgotten as he has been. He was the Constable of the Hundred of Stanborough for sixteen years.

Now the Constable's office is said to date back nearly 1,500 years and is based on a very simple principle of watch and defend, and that those immediately interested in taking care of their own safety and their own property were those who would be most likely to carry out the duties with assiduity.

Watch and defend describe the duties of the Constable; the times were very disturbed and night watch was kept for robbers and undesirables passing through the parish.

The onus of watching was laid on each parishioner, who was liable to be called to do duty, just as "The Special Constables" were in the great war. The price of liberty is perpetual vigilance.

In addition to the Constable of the Hundred there were one or two (Dean sometimes had two) petty (parish) Constables.

THE DUTIES OF THE CONSTABLE WERE :—

(1)   To see watch was kept in the watch house which was placed at some strategic point in the parish.

1594.   Pd to John Flynt towards the reparryng of the wach (watch) house.—xijd.

(2)   To take charge of all Weights and Measures in the

parish and see that they were stamped by the Clerk of the Market, who annually inspected them; there are references each year to a payment to him.

Weights and Scales are frequently inspected in these days by officials who pay surprise visits.

By the Statute of II Henry VIII. cap. iv., only certain towns were allowed to keep imperial standards. Totnes was the local town which kept the standard measures and where the Clerk of the Market lived. Corn measures were tested in the same way.

1574. Pd to the Clark of the Markyt (at Tottenes).—iiijs.

(3) To see that maimed soldiers received relief and attention and to see that the rate was collected for that purpose.

1594. Pd to the Constable of the Hundred towards relief of the maymed souldyoures for xiij weeks.—ijs. ijd.
　　Pd more for the same souldyoures at Christmas.—ijs. ijd.

(4) To collect the parish quota towards the upkeep of the local Gaol and Hospital.

1594. Pd to the Constable of the Hundred for the goele Michaelmas and Christmas quarters.—iijs. iijd.

Rates for the support and repairs of gaols, hospitals and assistance to maimed soldiers were collected quarterly by the Constable of the Hundred. Maimed soldiers were those wounded in the service of the State, to whom pensions were granted by the Act of 1593.

To see that the Parish Soldier was enlisted and duly equipped with his armour and weapons, or in emergencies that the parish quota of armed men was raised.

Another duty of the parish Constable was to preside at the stocks and whipping post. Beggars without a pass or licence to beg were taken to the whipping post and whipped, this was inflicted even on women and children. What savages our forefathers were.

1599. Pd to John Fox, Constable of the Hundred for martiallynge for Midsummer and Michellmas quarters.—xiijd.

(5) To see that the armour and weapons were all provided by the parish.

1570. Pd to the Constabell for his charges and travell to London and elsewhere for the optenynge of the sede armour.—vjs. viijd.

(6) To see that the Supervisors of the Wayes did their duty and repaired the roads. Dean was punished for neglect of the Roads.

1584. Pd to John Mudge allowed unto hym ijs. vjd. for part of the generall amersement (fine) for not reperynge of the wayes.

(7) To keep bridges in the Hundred in repair. Many are named in these accounts which are miles from Dean.

1572. Pd to the Constable for two bridges at Yampton.—6/4.
Pd for reparyng bridges between Blackawton & Halwell—10/8
Pd for re-edyfying of Thorneton Bridge.

(8) Escorting lawbreakers to Gaol.

Pd for carrying G. Williams to Gail.
1582. Pd to Mr. Franklyne (Constable) for brynging a prysoner to ye Jele.—iijd.

(9) Carrying lawbreakers before the justices. Every village had its lock-up or place of detention, this refers to the lock-up at Dean.

1579. Pd for expense towards the House of Correcssion (correction) iijs. iiijd.
Pd for a precept to call Christopher M. Mudge before Her Majestie's Justyces.—vjd.

(10) To report any default of the parish in keeping the Statutes of the Realm. Dean was fined for this in 1584.

1584. Pd to the High Constabell for wante of exercyon (exercising) the Statute of Archerye.—ijs. iijd.

(11) To bring men condemned to the gibbet. Dean has this startling record.

1582. Item pd to Mr. Franklyne (The Constable) for carynge of forynge (not Devon men) prysoners to be executyd here in the contre (country).—6d.

There is a record here that seems to show that these men were executed for highway robbery and murder. Six weeks before "a gentleman stranger" was murdered while passing through the parish and buried in Dean Churchyard.

Dean Court has for centuries been the principal house in the parish, and there are, or were, documents which contained detailed records of prisoners being tried for murder in the large hall, convicted and taken out and hanged.

The entry immediately preceding the one recording the executions is interesting.

1582. Pd to one drawn a feller.—4d.

The interpretation seems to be that one of the men executed was drawn and quartered—a barbarous practise quite common in those days, usually performed on the ringleader.

WELLSBROOK, HUNTINGDON WARREN.

THE LETTERS OF AN EXECUTIONER TO AN UNDERSHERIFF.

SIR,

In answer to your letter I have to inform you my father has been dead these two years past, and I have taken it upon me to execute the same office as my father did. I am engaged with the County——on the same terms as my father held it, and have the same salary as he recd from that county, I am not aware what my father recd from the county——for an Execution, but I have no objection to taking it on the same terms as he held it . . I know fcr some years past he had no regular salary from your county. From the county of——he had four pounds for the execution of a person and five pounds for the county of——.

If you will allow me five pounds for the execution of a person and my travelling expenses I have no objection of serving you and you may depend on me as you did on my father. You had no need to be afraid of my Executing the Office, as I have attended my father at executions at—— and it was his desire after his death for me to take the same office if accepted

I am, Your Obedt Servant—

To same as above :——

SIR,

I cannot give you a certificate from the Governor of—— as he is Dead, but you may depend on me without the least doubt that I am as capable of executing a Man as my Father.

I have never executed anyone but attended (as I told you on my Letter) and I have not the least shadow of a doubt but that I shall be able to execute the office to your satisfaction. If you will accept of my services, my age is thirty-six, my person as tall as my Father but stouter.

If the Undersheriff will accept of my services he may depend on my attending at the time appointed with timely notice.

I remain, Your Obedt Servt—

To Undersheriff : —

SIR,

As you wish to know my charge for coming down and the execution of the man, I cannot take less than Ten Pounds.

As you will please to consider my Situation it is not a very pleasant calling, my Father had a salary of Ten Pounds a year, I shall have none but the mony when a Execution takes place. As it now but seldom, and there might not be another in your County for years to come.

You have not told me where I am to put up when I come down. As I should wish to be as private as possible while I am there, I should consider the Prison to be the best place for me to reside while there, you will please to let me know by return of post. I shall not be able to arrange it to leave home untill Saturday in the morning by one or two o'clock. I shall walk to——and then take the fast train to ——and then a cab to take me to the place you will appoint.

I remain, Your Obedt Servt—

(12) Also the Constable of the Hundred had to see that the armour was in good order and ready for use.

In 1573 there is a list of the pieces delevered to **Mr. Arter** Champnowne for the pjyshe (parish) armoury, one callyver, one morryan,
one flaske, one toucheboxse, one mole, with the hangenes for the
same for the pjyshe the 5th daye of August anno dom 1573.

(13) Attending the Beacon. The Constable had to
see the beacons were properly made and lit at the right
time.

How busy the Constables of Devon must have been
both before and after the defeat of the Armada, when
beacons blazed on all the important hill-tops.

THE PARISH SOLDIER.

Each parish was required to train and arm a soldier for
60 days in a year in peace in readiness to serve at home
or abroad in war ; contribute a quota of trained men
according to the population of the parish, with their
armour which was to be kept in good order. The expenses of training and of attending the general muster fell
on the rates.

The plan was to raise in England 30,000 men to defend
the country against invasion. Of the 10,000 to defend
the coasts, 10,000 to defend London, the remaining
10,000 to be held in reserve to be thrown in wherever
they were wanted in emergency.

1598. Pd to the Captain for trayninge of our soldyer at Dipford.—
ijs.

His Equipment.

1573. What armour there was in anno dom. 1573 by the iiij men
for the pjyshe delevered to Mr. Arter Champnowne, one Callyver,
one morryan, one flaske, one toychboxse (touchbox), one mole with
its hangenes for the same for the pjyshe (parish) anew the 5 daye of
August Anno Dom 1573.

There are annual records of the training at Totnes,
Diptford, Rattery, &c.

1576. Pd for the trenynge of the soyederes at the last muster at
Tottenes.—ixs. xjd.   Item to the muster at Totnes.

His Panoply of War

on setting out on foreign service.

1573. Delevered unto Cryspen B for Irland by psepte (precept) one
sword, one dagger, one black bylle, one sword girdell anew, xvjth
daye of August, 1573.

Our Parish Soldiers for foreign service embarked at Plymouth.

1592. Pd to John Hele for his travel to Plymouth at several tymes with the sodyeres.—ijs. vjd.

His Friends.

Our Parish Soldiers had friends to think of their wants and comforts, as our soldiers had in the Great War.

1579. Pd for a soyderer cote —iiijs. vjd.
1590. Payed to Margery Downdege for flocks for the doblets Greta Forde made for the sodgers—iijd.

> *Doblets—a loose garment coming below the belt.*
> *Flocks—locks of wool.*

Greta Forde made warm woollen garments for the soldiers.

> " This flock of wool, and this rich locke of hair,
> This ball of cowslips, these gave me here."

> ROBERT HERRICK *in " A Pastoral sung to a King."*

And a great poet to encourage and counsel those who fought in the Civil War—an hitherto undiscovered poem. The following *hitherto undiscovered poem* evidently written by Herrick's own hand, vertically, on the margin of the page from bottom to top, in the 1585 account.

> " If that it chaunce the wares for to fight
> More then to witt truste, not to thy might
> For witt without strength, much more doth prevayle
> Than strength without witt to conquer in battell."

> ROBERT HERRICK. *Probably written about* 1630.

THE ARMOURY AND THE ARMOURER.

There are numerous references to the Armoury and the Armourer.

1570. Pd to James Willyames for neles, lether and buckeles for our harnes.—vjd.
1570.—For neles to hange uppe the Pekes.—jd.
1573. Pd for hangenes for the iiij Callyvers.—ijs.
1576. Pd to the Cuttelers for trymynge and dressing of our Armour.—iiijs.
1597. Pd for a skowerer for a collyver.—iiijd.

A Skourer was a mop or swab used to clean the bore of a Callyver between the discharges.

1572.   Pd to James Wyllyams for kepynge of the harness and Pd for large neles (nails) and other things for the armour.—ijs.
1574.   Pd for kepynge of the harnes, &c.—ijs. viijd.
1569.   Pd for scourynge of the Church harnes.—iijd.

Conveyance of the Armour.

1588. –Pd for carriage of our armour at severall tymes.—ijs. ijd.
   ,,   Pd for a horse for our armour in Tottenes.—xvjd.
1598.—Pd for standynge of our pish armour at Dipford and carrage.—xd.
1580.—Pd for a horse and carynge of the pjshe armor home from Exeter.—xd.
1596.—Pd to the Armourer the j daie of Maye and for a chape of a sword. - ij. iij.
1598.   Pd to the Armourer for makynge clean of the Armour and Pd for leather to make strapps for the armour.—iiijd.

RIVER AVON BELOW HUNTINGDON WARREN.
Photo by Capt. Stone.

ARCHERY.

In 1567, Commissioners of Archery were appointed to carry out a great revival in the use of the bow. The long bow long continued in use after the use of gunpowder for the small fire arms, and was used in the Civil Wars and later.

1569. Pd to John Mudge and John Gele for their expense to ride to Tottenes before the Quene's Instructors (in Archery).—viijd.

1574. Pd before the Queene's Commyoners.—ixd.

1577. Pd to the Comyshyoners for Archerye.—viijs.
       Pd to the High Constabell for wante of the exersyon (exercising of the statute of Archerye.—ijs. iiijd.

A " shefe " of arrows (24) could be bought from the Queen's store for xxd. Here is a record of a double quantity but at the same rate.

1573. Pd for a shefe of arroes.—iijs. iiijd.

1597. Pd to too that had a comyssion att Brent for the mentoninge of Artycherye according to the Statute in that case provided.—iijs.

GUNPOWDER.

The Archery Act of 1569 had only just come into force when the discovery was made that gunpowder could be used in small fire arms, and the great superiority of small guns charged with gunpowder over the bow and arrow.

We find the first mention of gunpowder in the Dean Accounts in the following year.

1570. Pd for halfe a pound of powder.—viijd.

Then soon follows the second mention of it :

1571. Pd for a pounde and a halfe of powder.—ijs.

After this it is purchased in quantities annually :

1596. Pd for a newe bagg for gonnpouder.—vjd.
,,   Pd for x lb. of gonnpouder the 13th April.—xijs. vjd.

The gunpowder and the armour were kept in the Church, the former with dire results to the Church in some parishes.

1567. Pd for scourynge (cleaning) the Church harnes.—iijd.

St. Columb Major, Basingstoke and Torrington were badly damaged by explosions. At Torrington the Church was destroyed and with it 200 prisoners who were imprisoned within its walls. At the time of the disaster General Fairfax was riding through the town, and when the Church was blown up a piece of lead fell close to his horse, the animal reared but Fairfax was not thrown off. The man at his side had his horse struck by lead and killed.

ARMS AND ARMOUR.

Allmayne-rivettes. A German coat of armour made flexible with rivets.

1585. Pd for the charge of one pere of Alman Revets.--viijs.

Byll. A concave battle-axe with long wooden handle.

Black Byll. One which had recently been ground and made ready for use.

1574. Pd for a blacke bylle.—ijs.

A *Brown Byll.* One which has become rusty.

A *Twibyll.* An awful weapon, like a pick-axe but with a kind of two-edged sword one side, balanced by a pole-axe the other. The warrior who missed his opponent with the two-edged sword side could, with a sharp turn of his wrist, pole-axe him.

A *Bage.* To keep the gunpowder or bullets in.

1588. Pd for too bagges for the pyllets.—iijd.
1596. Pd for a newe bage for gonnpouder.—vjd.

Cappe. A steel helmet to place under a morrion. Sometimes the plain steel helmet was used only.

1587. Pd for ij cappes to weare under morrans.—xjd.

Caliver. The regulation firearm of Elizabeth's reign.

1570. Pd for iiij Callyvers.—vli. vjs. viijd.

Corslet. Usually made of leather and used by men armed with a byll or a pike.

1570. Pd for ij corseletts.—vjs. viijd.
1584. Pd for mendynge and lynynge of a moryan and new letherynge of the lytle corselett.

Daggers In very common use.

1573. Pd for ij swordes and ij daggers.—xjs.

Hedd Pyce. A helmet.

1596. Pd for a hedd pyce more.—vjs. viijd.
1586. Pd for a hedd pyce for the pusche.—vijs.

Flaske. A large flask in which they carried the gun-powder.

1584. Pd for newe lether for too flaskes.
1596. Pd for 2 payre of strappes for the flaskes.—viijd.
1598. Pd for lether to make strappes for the armour.—iiijd.

Hangenes To hang the armour on; it was hung up in Church.

1573. Pd for hangenes for the armour.
  ,,   Pd to Wyllyam Phillepe for the neyles.—vjs. viijd.

RIVER AVON BELOW HUNTINGDON WARREN.

Mole or Molde.   For making bullets with.
>1580.   Pd for a molde
>1591.   Pd for vij lb of ledde and makynge of the pyllets.—xxijd.

Morion.   A helmet without beaver.

Musket.   A heavy gun which could not be fired accurately without a support or rest.
>1588.   Pd for one musket with ye small flaske, toucheboxse and rest.—xxxijs. viijd:

A Pike had a long shaft with a sharp pointed head.
>1570.   Pd for x pekes.– xxs.   They were bought in London.
>Pd for the carrage of the same pekes from London to Exeter.
>   „   „   all the sede armour from Exeter home—iiijs. viijd.

A Scourer.   (*see above.*)
>1588.   Pd for a new scourer.—ijs.

Touchbox.   A very small flask for the priming powder.
>1598.   Pd for ij gerdeles and ij daggers and a tuichbox.—iiijs.

Gerdell or Girdle.
>1579.   Pd for a sworde gerdell.—xs. jd
>1580.   Received of John Gele for one sword gerdell.—xs. jd.
>1580.   Received of Robert Furze for one sworde gerdell and one dagger.—iijs. ijd.   (Robert Furze bought his weapons).

THE ARMADA PERIOD.

The Constables' Accounts for 1586, 1587, 1588, are almost entirely devoted to records of purchasing weapons and the repair of them, but there are two records of great importance bearing on the same problem, the saving of the *home front* from starvation.

1586 was a terrible year of dearth, the worst since 1316. The crops failed through exceptionally bad weather. The corn did not ripen, there being no sun but dreadful rains, and in consequence there was famine. It is not surprising to find that there was great anxiety as to the food supply in view of the threatened invasion of the country by Spain, so we find that there was a survey of the corn next year.

1587.　Item pd for the bill of Instructions for the view of the corn. vjd.

Further, there was the danger of profiteering. To prevent this protection was sought under the Assize of Bread passed in 1580.

1587.　Pd for a bill of Instructions for the overseers of the Bread— xijd.

Under the Assize of Bread the standard of prices and the size of the loaves were fixed, to stop profiteers taking advantage of the considerable rise of prices due to the failure of the crops and to the impending naval war.

Three editions of such Assizes (Enactments) were issued in 1528, 1530 and 1580. In the reign of William IV. the Assize of Bread was repealed, circa 1836.

These enactments were often made in times of dearth, and the earliest date is as early as the times of the Magna Charta, 1215.

ASSIZE OF BREAD.

Among the docments of the borough of Marazion is the "Assize of Bread." It is a large parchment roll giving in columns the weight of loaves according to fixed tariff of prices. It is divided into sections, for small bread and larger bread. The former includes the penny loaf and the twopenny; the latter, the sixpenny, the twelvepenny, and eightpenny. The proper weight and price of each is fixed. This was in consequence of an Act authorising the corporations of towns to set an assize of bread. There was an Assize of bread in Penzance in 1686.

Too much bread is fattening so the poet writes :
    " Nor is it that thou keepest the stricter 'size (assize)
    So much for want as exercise."
            HERRICK in " A Country Life."

Photo by]   CORRINGDON BALL.   [*Mrs Mead*

THE YEARS PRECEDING THE ARMADA.

THE PREPARATIONS AT DEAN TO MEET THE SPANISH ARMADA.

A list of the armour and weapons purchased in 1586, 1587, 1588 to equip the men of this small parish will give some idea of the immense preparations in the south of England to defend England's shores against the attacks of Philip of Spain. The portion of the coast garrisoned by the Dean Soldiers was at Blackpool, near Dartmouth, where a number of huts (over 30) were built and maintained for years as the accounts show. These huts were built and kept in repair with money raised in the parish of Dean Prior.

In these years there are a number of references to Blackpool; these will all be found under the heading ' Blackpool page.'

1586.

Pd. for charge at the muster at Tottenes.—iiijs.

,, conveayon of our Soldyer at (to) Dartmouth.—iijs xd.

,, our soldyer's newe apparell.—xvs. vd.

,, too sworde gerdles.—xxijd.

Pd more to the justices for the charge of the sodyers.—xxs.

Pd for one newe corselett and the carrage of the same.—xxxs.

,, charges of the tynners.—xxxiijs. iijd.

,, a newe flaske and touchboxse.—iiijd.

,, the charge of our sodyers and carrage of our armour in Aprile laste paste at Tottenes.—vs. vjd.

Pd more for one pounde of gonnepouder and too lbs. matches.— xviijd.

Pd for expenses of our sodyers the xxiij of Maye.—iiijs. vd.

,, half a pounde of gonnepouder then.—viijd,

,, a newe lether for our flaske.—iiijd.

,, too newe morryenes.—viijs.

Pd to Robert Furze for his wages and carrage of *his* armour.—xxd.

,, Phe Stevenes ,, ,; armour.

,. Edward Windeatt ,, ,,

,, Wm. Gele for his wages.—viijd.

,, John Phe ,, ,, —viijd.

Pd for mendynge of a Callyver.—ijd.

,, a horse to put our armour on.—iijd.

,, the kepynge, mendynge and makynge clene of our armour.—vs.

,, oyle and neles for our armour.—ijd.

Pd more to the Justices.

,, ,, to Mr. Frankelyne (the Constabell).—iijd.

,, ,, spent at Tottenes.—vijd.

Pd for a copye of the Leuetennants orders.—iiijd.

Item to Perse for the discharge of unlawful games.—iiijd.

NOTE.—These heavy costs were met by loans of money by parishioners who had money, and by a subsidy by the State.

These entries refer to loans repaid :—

Pd to Henry Gele for money lent.—ixs.

,, John Furze ,, ixs.

,, William Arscott ,, vs.

,, Robarte Furze ,, xvjs. viijd.

Pd more to the Vecar ,, vijs. viijd.

Pd to Wm. Gele ,, ijs. vjd.

Pd more for expenses at the taxse of the subsedye.—ijs.

Repayed of the olde debt to John Mudge.—iijd.

1587.

Pd to Philipp Stevens for makynge clene of the common armour.—xijd.

,, for oyle for the same armour.—iiijd.

,, to John Gilberte's clarke the third daye of May towards the trayninge of the foryners.—xxvjs. viijd.

,, for ij cappes to wear under morrans.—xjd.

,, for mendynge of a sworde girdle.—jd.

,, unto Robert Foxe for foure dayes trayninge and for caridge of his armour and for bullets.—xxxjd.

,, to Robt. Foxe for mendinge of a flaske and making of a scourer.—vj.

,, for mendyinge of a Callin.—xviijd.

,, to Philip Stephen for his wages for fouer dayes trayninge and for caridge of his armour and for bullets.—xxj.

,, unto Edward Windyeat for ij dayes trayninge and caridge of his armour.—xijd.

,, unto Will Lyell for ij dayes trayninge.—viijd.

,, ,, John Philip ,, ,, —viijd.

,, for other expenses then.—ijs. viijd.

,, to the Constable of the Hundred towards the settynge furthe of the souldyers at Totnes the 14th daye of Marche, 1586. - xxxiijs.

,, for a copye of a precepte for the said muster.—iiijd.

,, for the bill of Instructions for *the view of the Corne*.—xijd.

,, for the bill of Instructions for the *ovseers of the Bread*.—xijd.

,, for leather for our armour.—vjd.

,, for ij sword girdles —xd,

,, iiij pound of gunpouder. —vs. viijd.

,, iiij pound of ledde.—vjd

,, to Philip Pearson for kepynge of the pushe armour for one half year ended a Midsommer laste.—ijs.

,, more at the delivery of the subside booke- —vjd.

,, more for the satisfaction of the parryshe debts.—vs.

The Armada Year.

1588.

Pd for the cuttynge of iiij swords and charges for the same.--xxs.

,, more for iiij newe daggers and ij swords.—xvijs.

,, more for v sworde gurdeles.—iiijs xd.

,, for mendynge of too flaskes and one touchboxse.

,, for one Calyver.—ijs.

,, for a newe Skouerer.—ijd.

,, for v lb. of gonnepouder.--vs. viijd.

,, for lede.--ixd.

,, for too bagges for the bullets.—iijd.

,, for v lb of maches.--ijs vijd.

,, for the carrage of our armour att several tymes.--ijs. ijd.

Photo by]   WM. HILL with drashel still in use.   [*Mrs. Mead*

Pd for a house for our armour in Tottenes.—iijd.
More pd for expenses at Tottenes.—xvjd.
Pd for one muskett and rest.—xxxijs.
  ,, charges at Kyngesbrygge for the clarke of the markytt.—ijs.
More pd to the trennynge of the tynners.—xd.
Pd for charges at Plymmouthe —vjd.
  ,, for kepynge of our armour.—iiijs.
  ,, for one pynte of yoayell (oil) for the armour.—vjd.

REPAYMENT OF BORROWED MONEY—Pd xxvs. money that the pusche did borrow, that is to saye to Robarte Furze vjs. viijd., to Henry Gele vjs. viijd., to John Gele ijs. xd,, to William Gele vjs. xiijd., to John Furze ijs. ijd.

Pd more for iij lb. of pouder, iijs. vjd., and for ij lb. of matches, viijd., and for more ledde, vjd.

In 1588, possibly at the very time the Armada was passing Plymouth, Robert Furze, the Constable of the Hundred paid a visit to the armoury and found some missing and was evidently told it had been taken by the iiij men. An order is given that when they brought it back it was to be put into the Church House. Then follows a list of the missing pieces – fyrste iij Corslets, j Allmayne Revet, a bylle, ij Callevers, j sword gerdell and iiij pyckes, and ij broken pyches and ij blacke morens and a musket and flaxe, and toucheboxe, and reste for the same.

The Defence of Blackpool.

1568.

The soldiers raised in Dean were sent to a scene of the landings of several invaders, Blackpool, near Dartmouth, to defend a section of the coast, and they built quite thirty wooden huts there (garres) and maintained them for years.

We find records of them years before the Armada panic.

In the early years of the reign of Queen Elizabeth her government strengthened the defences of the country : the navy was increased, munitions of war were stored in arsenals, and all along the coast weak points were fortified and the making of brass cannon and of powder were introduced and stored. It was known then that Philip of Spain was gradually building ships and assembling the engines of war.

These great outlays of money for defence of the country account for the Constables' Accounts being so full of purchase of arms and armour, 1569 to 1573. Here are a few entries : —

1570. Pd for iiij Callyvers.—vli vjs. viijd.
,,   carrage of the same from London to Exeter.—ijs. viijd.
,,   ij corseletes.—vjs. viijd.
,,   charge of same from London to Exeter.—vjs. viijd.
,,   one corselet.--iijs. iiij.
,,   for x pekes —xxs.
,,   carrage of same from London to Exeter.—vs.
,,   carrage of all the sede armour from Exeter home.—iijs. viijd.
,,   the Constabell for his charges and travell to London and elsewhere for the optenynge of the sede armour.—vjs. viijd.
,,   the hangenes for iiij Callyvers.
,,   for neles to hange uppe the pekes.—jd.
,,   other charges to Robert Furze.—ijs. iiijd.

The armour was bought by a parish loan.

Repayde of the lente money for the puysyon (purchasing) of armour.

Then follows a list of 20 names of the parishioners who had lent money to buy the parish armour and the money was repaid this year. The amount each man lent is given.

Also these strengthening of defences of our country early in Elizabeth's reign account for the mention of the visits to Blackpool so early.

1568.   More payed to Blackepole.—xiijs.
        Pd to John Phylypps for ryding to Blackpole.—viijd.
        Received for Constable Backe for the carrying of our men to
          Blackpole.—ijs.
1586.   Pd for the mendynge of xij garres (huts) at Blackpole.—
          xijs. ijd.
        ,, for the redynge of the letts there.—iiijs.
        ,, for maken of too newe garrets there.—xiiijd.
        ,, for a copye of the order of the same.—iiijd.
        ,, for expenses at severall tymes.—xxijd.

Sir John Hawkins.

1587.   Pd for mendynge of xiiij garretts at Blackpole.—iiijs.
        ,, for the bill of order for the garretts and other furniture
          at Blackpoule.—vjd.
        ,, to L. Hele & Wm. Hele for their expense at Blackpoule.—
          xxjd.
        ,, for mendynge of the guns and other furnitures at
          Blackpoule by force of a precept from the Constable of
          the Hundred.—viijs

Then follow a number of purchases of new weapons.
1588.   Pd for charges for Blackpole.—vijs. iiijd.
        ,, more for one muskett with his mole flaske toucheboxse
          and rest.—xxxvjs. viijd. (a considerable sum of money).

The musket was another name for the well-known
weapon of those days, the Harquebus (from Danish **haak**,
a hook, **bus,** a gun), it was a heavy gun which could not

be fired accurately without the support of a fork or rest. Hence the mention of a rest. This is the last entry referring to Blackpool. Note it is in the Armada year; it is so obvious why Dean men were sent there. Did this musket actually fire at the Armada? It probably did as it passed by the bay. Imagine the thrilling sight of the Armada in full sail, that is what the Dean men saw; they would not be likely to have remained silent, no doubt they saluted as the great fleet of Spain sailed by.

After the Armada.

The Armada Defeat was followed by a few years' peace except that the Queen sent an expedition into Brittany, which John Syng evaded.

In 1592 the Queen sent 4,000 English into Normandy to help the King of France besiege Rouen.

1592.   Pd towards the settynge forth of John Synge prest out of the Stannarye for Brytagne.—xxs.
        (This man showed the white feather and deserted).
        Pd for a precept to call John Synge before Her Majesties Justices.—vjd.
        Pd for the prest of John Symons.—iiijd.

In 1595 and the following years there were great preparations for war at Dean which were due to three causes.

(1).   THE IRISH REBELLION.

In 1595 the Earl of Tyrone rebelled and maintained his rebellion for *seven* years.

1596.   Pd for Irland service the 30th October. —xxviijs.
1597.   ,,   the Constable of the Hundred for Irland service.—xs.
          ,,   for Andrews for his license.—iijs. iiijd.
1598.   ,,   to John Fox the Constable of the Hundred for Ireland Service ij severall tymes.—xijs. vjd.

In March this year the Earl of Essex sailed for Ireland with an army of 20,000 foot and 2,000 horse against the Earl of Tyrone.

The Constables' Accounts for 1596 are very long owing to this expedition to Ireland to crush the rebellion.

Here are a few interesting entries :

Pd for the maken of the garretts (huts probably made of turf) at Blacke Podzeatt and expense.—xjs. iiijd.
   ,, more for pouder there and macken the Seatt.—xiijs.

Pd for 2 tymes to the fronte poste John Synge.—viijd.
,, for a newe bagg for gonnpouder.—vjd.
,, for 2 payre of strappes for the flaskes.—viijd.

There was a Military funeral there.

Pd for a shroude to cover the bodye of one dromner (drummer) at Collamytt Podzett.—ijs. jd.

Pd oute for X lb. of gonnpouder,—xijs. vjd.
,, for a hedd pyce more (a morion),—vjs. viijd.

The two places named are probably villages in Ireland, I cannot locate them. Note :—they built turf huts there so they evidently anticipated a long stay.

As the huts cost about 7d. each (turf would be on the spot) they must have built a good number, and evidently a fairly large contingent of Dean men took part in the expedition. John Synge was sent but I cannot trace that our timid parishioner, the Tinner, ever returned.

There are many entries in the Accounts which show that Ireland was very restive in Tudor times. I give two entries :

1570. Pd for the settynge forthe of the soldyers into Ireland.—xxxvjs. viijd.
1583. Pd when ye fourners (foreigners) went into Ireland —vjs. xjd.

Photo by]   GLAZE WOODS.   [*Mrs Mead*

(2). THE EXPEDITION TO THE WEST INDIES.

The second cause was that Queen Elizabeth sent Sir John Hawkins and Sir Francis Drake on an expedition against the Spanish Colonies in the West Indies.

We hear much about the triumph over the Armada, but we hear nothing of the tragedy of this voyage. A pathetic entry in Dean register throws some light on it. There was a shortage of men as well as ships, and a Dean man was prest for service.

1595. Item there was dellevered to Robert Bonethon beynge prest for Syr John Hawkens and Syr Frances Dracke ; then follows the details of his armour––of the purreshes armor one hedd pyce one sworde one dagger and one gerdell the 28th of August 1595.

Note the date––for on November 12th Sir John Hawkins died, and on January 28th following Sir Francis Drake died.

The sailors and troops were decimated by disease to which both the Admirals succumbed, and the ships had to return home. In this expedition Drake staked the greater part of his fortune to provide ships which the Queen always stinted him.

Space prevents me telling the story of this sad event near the close of Elizabeth's reign.

The Dean soldier did not return.

(3). THE EXPEDITION TO CAPTURE CADIZ.

The third reason for these great preparations for war was that the Queen ordered an Expedition under Lord Howard of Effingham, with a large army under the Earl of Essex, to capture Cadiz, which they accomplished with ease and shattered the Spanish fleet in harbour ; the Spaniards, in their panic fled, and left Cadiz to the mercy of the enemy.

During this period Dean soldiers took part in the defence of the fort of Plymouth.

1597. Pd to John Foxe the Constable of the Hundred for the kepynge of ye fort of Plimoth and other service—viijs.

Queen Elizabeth's Visit to Dean.

EVIDENCE : —

(1) There is a very strong and clear tradition that Queen Elizabeth while passing through Dean stayed a night at the Giles mansion – Dean Court.

This is highly probable as Dean is situated on the main road from London to Plymouth, whither she would go to visit her Fleet. She was a great gadabout and it is not likely she would have left uninspected the great preparations of her Fleet for the coming of the Armada which had created such a panic through the country. I think she visited it in 1587, the year before the Armada. In 1587 there is a Special Rate for "*the Service of the Queen*" to which 35 Rate Payers contributed. In the Receipts of the Account is another rate, the usual parish rate. The Queen's Rate realised £5 10s. 4d. In this year Sir Francis Drake and Lord Howard of Effingham were making great preparations at Plymouth with the Fleet.

Her 2nd Visit.

She possibly visited it also in 1597.

(1) Her favourite, the Earl of Essex was assembling his forces to attempt the capture of Cadiz, which he succeeded in doing.

He sailed from Plymouth June 1st, 1597.

(2) In 1597 this entry occurs twice :—

Pd to John Fox Constable of ye Hundred for the Purvayers.—iijs.

Purveyor was used as a technical term for the caterers for the Queen's provisions.

Previous to 1592 the Queen's price for her food was fixed, which was always much less than the market price, the loss fell on the parish, and is mentioned in the Constables Account,

In 1592 a law was passed fixing an amercement on each parish, so that the total sum was distributed over all parishes in the neighbourhood. Hence the smaller amount iijs.

As it occurs again, it seems that the Queen halted at Dean on her forward journey to Plymouth, and on her return.

(3)   Then in 1597 this entry occurs twice :—
Pd to too that had the Queene's Broad Seale.— xd.

This unquestionably refers to the Great Seal of the Realm, and why is it mentioned, and what use was it put to on this occasion?

Photo by]   WISHING POOL.   [*Mrs. Mead*

TINNERS.

In the reign of Elizabeth the valleys of Dartmoor were being explored by tinners who streamed the stream beds and turned the soil of the valleys over and over again in search of tin. Some of the Dartmoor rivers' valleys are scored by the heaps they have left behind them, and the hills seamed with their workings as at Challacombe, as seen from Headland Warren.

The tinners pursuing their lonely quest among the Dartmoor hills were not exempt from military service. The state had no power to call them up to compulsory military service, but the Stannery Court had. Here are some references to the Tynners having " to join up " and defend their country.

1569.   Pd for Clyste (oil) for our drylles worke, (drilling rock)—iiijs.
     ,, for the charge towards my Lorde Warden's man and for expenses.—iiijs.   (Lord Warden of the Stannaries).
1574.   Pd to John Gilbertes for the Tynners bookes.—ijs.·
     ,, at the Musteres.—xijd.

1575.   Pd for the prest money of the tinners.—xxd.
1581.   Pd for Archery for tynners.—js. iiijd.
1586,   Pd for the benyvolens (benevolence) and other charges of
      the tynners.—xxxiijs. iijd.
1587.   Pd to the Bayliff of the Stannarie at ij several tymes.—xijd.
    ,,   for our bill of armour for the tynners.   xijd.
    ,,   to the Clarke (of the Markyt) for receavinge of our bill.—
      vjd.
    Owen to Mr. Francklyne's man for the tinners.—vjd.
    Pd to the raters towards the traynynge of the tinners.—xd.
1588,   ,,   for the trenynge of the tynners.—xd.
1592.   Pd towards the settynge forth of John Syng prest out of
      the Stannarye for Brytagne.—xxs. (This man was
      possibly a Conchy and evidently shirked the duty of
      defending his country).
    Pd for a precept to call John Syng before Her Majesty's
      Justices.—vjd.
1596.   Pd at the mustre for the tyners, and for my expenses
      tarrynge there one night.—ijs.
1597.   Pd to John Gele the elder the 16th of October for the
      tenners'—vjs. viijd.
1598.   Pd for vj trayned Tynners and for one day's trayninge at
      Bockefastlee.—iiijs.
    ,,   to the iiij Ratters (raters) of the Stannerye Cort at
      Ashburton for the Tynners.
    ,,   to John Hutt the tyne bailife for prest tinners.—xxs. vjd.
    ,,   for the trayning of 7 tynners for V dayes at 9d. a
      daye.—vs. iijd.

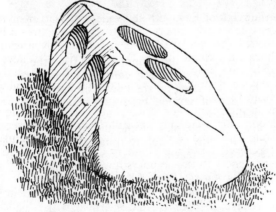

TIN MORTAR STONE ON GLAZEBROOK.
From a Drawing by Mr. R. Hansford Worth.

Relief of the Poor of the Parish and Poor Wayfarers.

This was a duty which was a legal liability of every Parish and appears in the Constables, Churchwardens and Collectors for the Poor Accounts.

All poor Travellers had to be relieved at the expense of the parish, provided they had a pass to permit them to beg; if they begged without a Pass they were taken to the whipping post and whipped.

Photo by]   Glazecombe.   *[Mrs. Mead*

Dreadful poverty resulted immediately from the dissolution of the Monasteries, and continued for years, and inflicted much suffering on the poor who have usually to bear the burden of national calamities which bring great poverty on the land.

Here are few examples of the unfortunate folk who were down and out, and had to tramp the roads and eke out a precarious existence.

The Relief of Poor Travellers.

This was a duty and legal liability of every parish; they were to relieve all poor travellers armed with a pass or permit to ask for relief and formed one of the duties of the Parish Constable; sometimes the entries occur in the

Churchwardens' and Collectors' of the Poor Accounts. If they came without a pass and begged they were whipped.

One of the results of the Dissolution of the Monasteries was great poverty all over the land, many people were utterly ruined.

Here are a few examples of the unfortunate folk who were down and out and who had to tramp the roads to eke out a precarious existence.

1567 Pd to fore maymed soder (soldier) men.—xs.
1572   ,, to a pore man of Torynton.—iijd.
1584   ,, to a poore man that gathered on ye Kingesbrydge.—iiijd.
1585   ,, to too pore men.—vjd.
1587   ,, to dyvers poore men at severall tymes.—iijs.
       ,, to fyftene pouer men at iijd. a man.   iijs. ixd.
1592   ,, unto men that gathered under the Queen's Authoritye several tymes.—ijs. xjd.

Photo by]   GLAZE COMBE.   *[W. R. Gay*

1594   Pd to a poure woman. — iijd.

1595   ,, to viij pouer men that haf severall licences to make
Collections. ijs. xd.

1597   ,, to a poore boye.—ijd.
,, to a poure woman.—iiijd.
,, to a woman and a chylde that was sent from tything to
tythinge.—iijd.
,, to the Constable of the Hundred towards the relyfe of the
pouer of Paynton by order of the Justices.—xs. (evidently
the quota of the parish were required to pay towards
special distress at Paignton).

1599   ,, to ij soldyers that came from Ireland. — iijd.
,, to a pouer woman from Cornwall that came to ye church.-jd
,, to Mr. Curtese (the Constable) towards the relefe of
vaccabonds this yere.—xvd.
,, for meamyed sayllers.—viijd.

CONTENTS.

GLAZECOMBE CORNER.

Photo by]   EAST GLAZE.   [W. R. Gay

Photo by]   WATERSLIDE, DEAN BOURN.   *[W. R. Gay*

SOME DARTMOOR WORTHIES.

WILLIAM GYLES, Gentleman, of Bowden near Totnes, father of John Gyles, in the middle of the 16th century purchased the Manor of Dean from Henry VIII, together with the advowson of the living of Dean. William was Churchwarden of Dean 1563, and one of the iiij men in 1565. He was buried at Dean.

(For full information about the Gyles family, see Prince s "Worthies of Devon.")

ROBERT FURZE, of Moreshead. (See my book " ROBERT FURZE, Gentleman," pub. Feb. 1932.)

JOHN GYLES, Gentleman, LORD OF THE MANOR OF DEAN PRIOR : - Built Dean Court which was a fine house in its early days. He was one of iiij men of Dean in 1582,— the executions year.

He was Churchwarden of Dean in 1587, the year before the Armada, when the growing corn in the parish was surveyed after the Famine year of 1586. He was suc-ceeded at Dean Court by his son, Sir Edward Gyles.

MARGERY MUDGE, CHURCHWARDEN OF DEAN, 1560 — Margery was a very good woman and a pillar of the Church, who did much in her day to support the work of the Church and the many activities of the parish. She survived her husband.

Margery Mudge, widow, was buryed ye ij August, 1578. In the Churchwarden's Accounts - received for Margery Mudge's grave in the Church, vjs. iiijd.

The final reference to her is pathetic :—

1578. Margery Mudge's gift to the poure.—iijs. iiijd.

ROBERT TOLCHARD, KEEPER OF THE BELLS :—

1596. Pd to Robert Tolchard for kepynge of the bells.—ijd.

Robert was a very faithful man and very devoted to the Church through Queen Elizabeth's reign, and for a great many years held the honourable Office of Keeper of the Bells. He had a brother John, who also did much work for the Church.

SIR EDWARD GYLES, KNIGHT, was born in 1576. He trailed a pike for the Queen for several years in his earlier years, in the Low Countries, then the scene of war. After James I ascended the Throne he became a great favourite at the Court, and although so young, was knighted by the King at the Coronation in 1604. After his father's death he lived in great state at Bowden, near Totnes, and was elected M.P. for Totnes in every election in the reign of James I, and Charles 1., until his death in 1637.

He was buried in the South Aisle of Dean Church, and above in the wall is placed a fine monument. The child is an adopted son, who died young.

ROBERT HERRICK is the Devon poet-vicar, who was vicar of Dean Prior, 1629 to 1674, although during the Commonwealth he was turned out of his living, and an intruder took his place for a few years, but the Restoration saw him return.

He has been described as the sweetest lyric who sang in the 17th Century. Born in Cheapside in 1591, he was a Londoner, and was soon an orphan, as his father died a little more than a year after he was born, having, like

Given January 1926
by Lovers of Dean Prior
and of Robert Herrick Poet.

ROBERT HERRICK.

ROBERT HERRICK.

Eutychus, fallen from an upper story and was taken up
dead. His mother, soon after his father's death, left
Cheapside with her seven children, and an eighth was
soon after born, and settled in Hampton-on-Thames.
Robert Herrick was sent to Westminster School. He, in
due course, was sent to Trinity Hall, Cambridge, where

he graduated B.A., in 1617, and M.A. in 1620. Herrick took Holy Orders in 1629, and in the same year was presented by Charles I. to the living of Dean Prior. Of this change in his life he writes : —

> " It is not need
> But 'tis the God of nature who intends
> And shapes my function for more glorious ends."

He seems to have travelled to Devon by sea, from London to Plymouth. In the " Hesprides," his greatest work, we find a series of delightful pictures of Herrick's life at Dean Prior. Dean Prior in Herrick's day, before the era of railways and motor buses, was rather isolated, and Herrick felt the isolation, yet it was good for him and his work, as he confessed more than once in the same breath with which he began to grumble :—

Photo by   DEAN BOURN.   *W. R. Gay*

> " More discontents I never had
> Since I was born, than here ;
> Where I have been and am still am sad
> In this dull Devonshire.
> Yet justly too, I must confess
> I ne'er invented such
> Ennobled numbers for the press
> Than where I loath'd so much."

Many of his poems were the product of this quiet life. He is considered to be the author of " Poor Robin's Almanack," first published in 1661.

He died at Dean Prior in 1674, at the age of 84, and was buried in the Churchyard or in the Chancel, but the place of his sepulchre is unknown to this day.

Photo by]　　　RIVER ERME.　　　[*W. R. Gay*

He was a bachelor and lived with an old housekeeper, Pru, in the lower part of the present vicarage, his simple lonely life with this old servant forms the theme of several of his poems. She was buried in 1678.

To Herrick's brain and industry we owe the preservation of the wonderful records 1567-1600. He evidently found the pages loose sheets. He was quick to see their value, and with great industry sewed them together with fine string and thick thread in a rough way, – just as a man would do it.

At the end he writes his confession of belief :—

> " Thou art my God and Saviour
> One Whom I awaite allwayes."

THE POET'S CORNER.
Gems from Herrick.

Herrick's Confession of his faith (written about 1635).
"Thou art my God and Saviour
One Whom I awaite allwayes."

Upon Prue, his Maid.

In this little urn is laid
   Prudence Baldwin (once my
   maid),
From whose happy spark here let
   Spring the purple violet.

Upon Prudence Baldwin, her sickness.

Prue, my dearest maid is sick
Almost to be lunatic:
Æsculapius! come and bring
Means for her recovering,
And a gallant cock shall be
Offered up by her to thee.

Photo by]   HERRICK'S VICARAGE. [*W. R. Gay, S. Brent*

A Thanksgiving to God for his House.

Lord, Thou hast given me a cell
   Wherein to dwell;
A little house, whose humble roof
   Is waterproof.

Under the spars of which I lie
   Both soft and dry,

Where Thou, my chamber for to
   ward,
   Hath set a guard
Of harmless thoughts, to watch
   and keep
   Me while I sleep.

Low is my porch as is my fate,
  Both void of state :
And yet the threshold of my door
  Is worn by th' poor,
Who thither come and freely get
  Good words or meat.

Like as my parlour, so my hall
  And kitchen's small,
A little buttery, and therein
  A little bin
Which keeps my little loaf of
  bread
    Unchipped, unflead ;
Some brittle sticks of thorn or
  briar
    Make me a fire,
Close by whose living fire I sit
  And glow like it.

Lord, I confess too, when I dine,
  The pulse is thine,
And all those little bits that be
  There placed by Thee ;
The worts, the purslane, and the
  mess
    Of water-cress,
Which of Thy kindness Thou
  hast sent,
    And my content ;

Make those, and my beloved beet
  To be more sweet.

Lord, 'tis Thy plenty-dropping
  hand
    That soils my land,
And giv'st me, for my bushel
  sown,
    Twice ten for one ;

Thou mak'st my teeming hen
  Her eggs each day,
Besides my healthful eyes to
  bear
    Me turns each year,
The while the conduits of my
  kine
    Run cream for wine.

All these, and better Thou dost
  send
    Me, to this end,
That I should render, for my
  part
    A thankful heart.
Which, fired with incense I resign
  As wholly Thine,
But the acceptance, that must
  be
    My Christ, by Thee.

To Electra.

More white than whitest lilies far,
Or snow, or whitest swans you
  are :
More white than are the whitest
  creams,
Or   moonlight   tinselling   the
  streams.

To Ben Johnson.

Make the way smooth for me
When I, thy Herrick,
Honouring thee, on my knee
I offer my lyric.

To Lady Carew, upon the death of her child.

Why, Madam, will ye longer weep,
Whereas your baby's lulled asleep.
And, pretty child, feels now no more
Those pains it lately felt before.
All now is silent ; growns are fled ;
But rather, like a flower hid here,
To spring again another year

Upon Mistress Suzanna Southe, her feet.

Her pretty feet
Like snails did creep
A little out, and then
As if they playéd at bo-peep,
Did soon draw in again.

Compare.

Suckling upon a wedding

" Her feet beneath her petticoat
Like little mice, stole in and out
As if they feared the light."

Herrick's Hesperides.
i—79.
To Julia.

Julia, when thy Herrick dies,
Close thou up the poet's eyes :
And his last breath, let it be
Taken in by none but thee.

— —

Dearest, bury me
Under that Holy Oak, or Gospel Tree,
Where (tho' thou sees't not) thou mayest think upon me,
When thou yearly goest in procession (*Rogation Procession*).

These lines on " A Ring " presented to Julia beautifully describes the symbolical character of the plain gold ring.

"And as this round
Is nowhere found
To flaw, or else to sever ;

So let our love
As endless prove
And pure as gold for ever."

O Dartmoor, My Dartmoor.

O Dartmoor ! how I love you, with your heather and your hills
Your rocky tors, your peaty bogs, your little singing rills !
I love to feel your mystery, to watch your changing moods,
To read your age-old history in stones and wayside Roods !
O land of light and shadow, glowing colour, veiling mist,
I hear you ever calling me, and how can I resist ?
I gaze with longing heart towards your hills of dreamy blue,
Across the dreary valleys keeping me apart from you.

In far-off years behind us, when mankind had time to dream
And think of all the real things   not things that only seem—
The Islands of the Blest were then their hearts' true place of rest ;
But Dartmoor is my Homeland, where my heart has made her nest.

Yes, Dartmoor is my Dreamland, lying purple in the West,
The land I love the best, all gold and purple in the West,
The haven of my spirit, and my Kingdom of the Blest !
Then draw me, ancient mother, to your wild but loving breast !

Marjory Barrett Fielden.

This verse was found inside a Prayer Book in Dean Prior Church some years ago.

" Steal not this book for very shame
For here you see the Owner's Name,
And when you die the Lord will say
" Where is that Book you stole away,"
And if you say you cannot tell,
The Lord will cast you down to Hell.

Field Names of Dean Prior.

Abrahams Meadow
Higher Addish
          Meadow
Lower Addish
          Meadow
Balldown
Bank
Baker
Higher Bakers
Barrow Meadow
Barter's Field
Bennet's Park
Big Meadow
Bidon's Park
Bedda
Bunkers'-close
Long Blackwells
Brake
Brimpark
Broadpark
Broom-park
Bush
Churchway Meadow
Church-field
Clapper Close
Higher Clerk's
Lower   ,,
Cockshell Barn
Colly Park
Conyeat Meadow
Crooked Down
Cross
Daisies Park
Delicate
Dean Park Barn
          Field
Edmonds-hill
Eight Acres
Flat-field
Fogen's
Foredown
Fox's Barn Field
French Park

Fuzzy-hill
Fuzzy Park
Golden Caps
Gran-hill
Great Clampit
Grey Down
Green
Grove Bewdown
Gutter-park
Happy
Harvest-park
Long Head
Higher-middle
Hix's Meadow
Hollow-greap
Holly Park
Home Bridge
Hood Park
Horse Field
Hull Park
Kealdown
Kiln Park
Kiln Close
Knackers-mead
Latta-barn
Lince Park
Little Mash
Longapark
Lower Long Down
Long Down
Long Rowden
Maddock's Down
Marles' Park
Marsh
Mash
Meshett's Hill
Mitchell's
Nap
New Park
Newtake
Nurston Park
Out Park

One Hill
Old Warren
Outside Field
Higher Oxes
Lower Oxes
White Oxen.
Peek Gate
Plain Park
Pit Park
Pit Field
Pool Broadland
Robin's Hill
Pigs-i-bottom
Sanctuary
Sandhills
Sand Park
Sentry
Little Sentry
Shepherds
Shim Park
Sheeplinhay Mash
Slate Quarry
Square Field
Strawberry Close
Stidston
Strayer Park
Strowel
Stockland
Skerraton Pound
Sycamore
Tank
Ten Acres
Three Corners
Vicarage-meadow
Great Warraton
Wheat Park
Whitagrass
Wild Down
Water Park
Willmott's Meadow
Wood Park
Yonder-hill Field

For others see 'Skerraton Manor' in my book "Robert Furze, Gentleman," (published March, 1932.)

For the list of Morwenstow Field Names see the Author's book "MORWENSTOW."

Bullaven Golf Links.

Established 1828.

PIANOS

ALLISON
BECHSTEIN
HOPKINSON
MORLAND
ROGERS
STECK
STEINWAY

TURNER & PHILLIPS, L^{TD.}

MIDDLE OF GEORGE STREET

PLYMOUTH.

The Piano Specialists.

Part 11

South-West

The
Forest of Dartmoor

PART 2.—SOUTH-WEST.

With some Ancient Records of Dartmoor Parishes and of Dartmoor Worthies.

From a Sketch by]   SHEEP'S TOR.   *[Mr. Charles Brittan.*

By the Rev. H. HUGH BRETON, M.A.

(Rector of Meshaw, near South Molton).

Author of "Beautiful Dartmoor," "The Breezy Cornish Moors," "Land's End and the Lizard," "The North Coast of Cornwall," "Morwenstow," "Hawker of Morwenstow," The Heart of Dartmoor," "The Word Pictures of the Bible," "The Great Blizzard of Christmas, 1927," "The Great Winter on Dartmoor, 1928-29," "Spiritual Lessons from Dartmoor Forest," "White Heather" and "Crystal Streams," &c.

PRICE 1/-   Postage 2d.

NEW DARTMOOR BOOK

by the Rev. H. HUGH BRETON, M.A.,
(RECTOR OF MESHAW).

"The Forest of Dartmoor"

PART 1 - - **SOUTH-EAST.**

with Special Articles on "Some Ancient Records of Dartmoor Parishes," and on "Some Dartmoor Worthies," and each part will also contain a Poet's Corner. Part I. records a hitherto unknown poem of Robert Herrick's on the "Parish Soldier." p. 52, and a simple confession of his faith, p. 78.

Beautifully Illustrated. **Price 1/-** **Postage 2d.**
PART 2 — NOW READY.

The Books named below can still be procured from the Author.

Spiritual Lessons from Dartmoor Forest.
Part 1. **"White Heather"** and other studies.
Part 2. **"Crystal Streams"** and other studies.

All price 1/- each. Post 1½d.

The Heart of Dartmoor. Price 1/6 Post 2d.
(North-East and Centre).

The Dartmoor Snowstorm. Price 1/6. Post 2d.
(The Great Blizzard of Christmas, 1927).

A Great Winter on Dartmoor—(1928-29) with accounts of the unprecedented snowstorm at Dean Prior of February 16th, 1929, and the Great Ice Storm of the closing days of February. Price 1/- Post 1½d.

Word Pictures of the Bible - - Price 1/-

ALL these books can be purchased from :
Rev. H. HUGH BRETON,
Meshaw Rectory,
South Molton, N. Devon

The Forest of Dartmoor.

PART 2—SOUTH-WEST.

By the Rev. H. HUGH BRETON,

M.A.

(Rector of Meshaw, S. Molton).

PRINTED & PUBLISHED BY
HOYTEN & COLE,
39, WHIMPLE STREET, PLYMOUTH.
1932.

BEDFORD HOTEL

TAVISTOCK.

THE BEDFORD HOTEL, an imposing castellated Gothic building in the centre of the town, was erected about 1720 by Wriothesley, the third Duke of Bedford, for an occasional residence. It occupies a portion of the site of the Ancient Abbey, part of the refectory of which still remains, and which the Proprietor is pleased for his visitors to see, The Hotel is now replete with all modern requirements, for the comfort and convenience of visitors ; including Hot and Cold water in every bedroom. Central heating. Officially appointed by the Royal Automobile Club and the Automobile Association.

A charming adjunct is the delightful **Old Garden covering two acres.**

The extensive hotel yard is provided with excellent Garage accommodation. Posting in all its branches is done from here, and cars are let on hire.

Tavistock is by its geographical situation incomparably the most convenient centre in Devon and Cornwall for motoring and touring generally. Motorists making it their headquarters can visit any part of the two counties and return within the day, thereby avoiding the discomfort and waste of time in the packing which is involved in a continual change of habitation.

Salmon and Trout fishing, Golf (18 holes), Tennis, Croquet, Bowls, Hunting and Badminton in the winter.

UNDER PERSONAL SUPERVISION.

W. I. LAKE Proprietor.

TO

HIS ROYAL HIGHNESS,

EDWARD, PRINCE OF WALES,

AND

DUKE OF CORNWALL,

THIS DESCRIPTION OF HIS FOREST OF DARTMOOR,
DEVON.

Is humbly dedicated by the gracious permission of

𝕳𝖎𝖘 𝕽𝖔𝖞𝖆𝖑 𝕳𝖎𝖌𝖍𝖓𝖊𝖘𝖘 𝕻𝖗𝖎𝖓𝖈𝖊 𝕰𝖉𝖜𝖆𝖗𝖉,

MASTER FORESTER,

AND LORD WARDEN OF THE STANNARIES,

BY HIS LOYAL, FAITHFUL, AND MOST OBEDIENT SERVANT

H. HUGH BRETON.

Meshaw Rectory, Devon,
  July 1st, 1931.

PREFACE.

I offer this little book to the public, the second part of a series of four on " The Forest of Dartmoor," hoping it will enable visitors and others to know more of this delightful playground.

All the profits will be devoted to Church Work.

I thank these friends warmly : —

Mr. Charles Brittan, the Dartmoor artist, for the drawing for the Cover.

Mr. H. W. Harding for his pen and ink sketches.

Mr. Hansford Worth for his photos.

Messrs. Martins, Ltd., for the Rajah photos.

To the Western Morning News for allowing me to publish their photo of Mr. Pengelley's Funeral.

Mr. H. J. Crook for his excellent photo of Shavercombe Falls.

Mr. C. C. Calmady for notes on the First Rajah and for the photo of Harry Terrell.

H. HUGH BRETON.

MESHAW RECTORY,
  SOUTH MOLTON,
    June 1st, 1932.

Photo by]   SHAVERCOMBE FALLS.   [*Mr. H. J. Crook.*

Forest of Dartmoor

PART 2.

CHAPTER I.

THE UPPER VALLEYS OF THE ERME AND YEALM

I. 1. **Motor to Harford Church,** there leave your car at the schoolhouse on the south side of the Church, take lane R. which leads to Harford Gate which opens on the moor. Here take the path which leads north.

Just before reaching **Lower Piles** is a **Kistvaen** just before the stream, a feeder of the Erme, is reached. It has no Capstone but it is a good monument. It is 150 yards S. S.E. angle of Lower Piles enclosure. Measurements— 3 ft 7 in. long, 1 ft. 4 in. wide S. end, 2 ft. North end, depth 3 ft., 100 ft. S.E. stands a large stone, 110 ft. away from the Kistvaen is a small cairn 20 ft. diameter, the Kistvaen formerly covered by the cairn is now gone. The containing circle has seven stones still standing, diameter 15 ft.

2. **Higher Piles Wood** is a good specimen of an ancient Dartmoor Wood. (See Part I., p.p. 37, 39).

3. Keeping to the East side of the Erme in three miles **Brown Heath** is reached, here is an interesting group of remains.

A Kistvaen stood at the head of the stone row, but now it is muddled in the stones of the Cairn.

The Stone Row is double, and the circle at its north end; the row does not point to the centre of the circle, and the Cairn does not occupy the true centre of the circle, 90 ft. south of the curve the row touches another circle which lies on its east side. 450 ft. further south, the row touches and is partly lost in the wall of a pound which is on its west side. The pound encloses hut circles and it is unusual to find a pound wall interfering with a stone circle, and thus indirectly with an interment, since the row terminated in a Cairn formerly covering a Kistvaen.

Leaving Brown Heath regain the china clay railway line and follow it up to its termination.   Here we are close to Huntingdon remains.   (See Part I., p. 23).

I. 4.   **Red Lake Clay Works** cover a lot of ground and have been worked considerably.   Huge heaps of clay spoil the moor.   At the house of the head man one seems to be on the roof of the world – so high.   From here is swamp in every direction, so be careful how you pick your way. A train still leaves Bittaford once a day and returns in the evening, but like everything just now clay is hit rather hard.

I. 5.   Now back to Harford Bridge.   Here on the west side is a path which leads up to **Tristis Rock**.   Follow this up to Tristis Rock, on the south side of which is a fine group of remains.

Yadsworthy Stone Row runs N. and S., terminating in south end in a circle which has been the retaining circle of a barrow; this is S.W. of Tristis Rock, and between it and the Rock is the retaining circle of another barrow enclosing a ruined Kistvaen, the latter circle is very perfect and consists of 12 stones, diameter 16 ft., and is very regular. Of the Kistvaen only south side remains ; there is no trace of the other stones or capstones.

I. 6.   **Bullaven**.   Standing at Tristis Rock on the opposite side of the valley is Bullaven Farm Hotel, here one may stay and thoroughly enjoy the surrounding moor. The equipment is very up-to-date, and the charges reasonable.

I. 7.   From Tristis Rock continue two miles north, gaining the high ground.   The Tumulus is **Hillson's Hut** named after a man named Hillson, who made his home there for years.   The Cairn is surrounded by **an earth Circle** instead of stone.

I. 8.   Half-a mile W. of Hillsons Hut is **Stall Moor Row** a very fine stone row with large stones, it can be seen a great distance away.

I. 9.   **Beehive Hut** on the Erme.   If from the stone row you go on in a N. direction, in less than one mile you come down into a small lateral valley of the Erme, quite near the Erme in this little valley is a beehive hut, which was no doubt used by the Tinners in Elizabethan times.

I. 10 **Erme Valley Stone Row**. A mile north from the beehive hut is a circle, 42 ft diameter, with stones. From the circle starts the longest stone row in the British Isles. It runs uphill and down dale for $2\frac{1}{3}$ miles and terminates in the Cairn on the top of Green Hill; most of the stones as it ascends Green Hill are lost, either sunk in the bossy soil or taken away. The Row crosses the Erme half mile below Red Lake and then begins its ascent of Green Hill.

I. 11. **Erme Head**. From Red Lake the Erme may easily be followed up to Erme Head where are many tinner's heaps, the remains of considerable workings about here.

CHAPTER II.

CORNWOOD.

II. 1. **Hawns and Dendles**. is a great resort of Plymouthians for a day's outing or an afternoon ramble, and is reached by going to Coombe, from there take the footpath up the valley which runs just above the Yealm (part I., IX., 4); or to North Hele Farm and keep straight on until the road is reached at Dendles Green. From this point after crossing the river, Broadall Lake may be ascended.

In about half mile an old wall will be reached, cross it, and in 200 yards cross a second wall; here you will be out on the open moor; from here it is easy to follow the Broadall Lake up the Broadall Gulf to the stream's source under Pen Beacon. Just before a third wall is reached, are the remains of a prehistoric settlement with its Pounds and Hut Circles (part I., IX., 7). At Broadall Hut is swampy ground.

II. 2. Dendles Waste Circle. (See part I., IX , 7).

II. 3. **Stall Moor Stone Row** is 1,200 ft. long. (See I., 8). From Cornwood go to Wisdom Mill then on past Tor, keep right away from the river, about one mile you come to the open moor, here ascend the hill to the Row. Not

STONE ROW ON STALL MOOR.

far from the north end is a small stone circle in the Row. This Row should be seen by all Dartmoor visitors.

II. 4. **Pen Beacon** is reached from Cornwood by going to West Rook Farm and from there follow the lane to West Rook Gate which opens on to the moor; from here ascend.

Pen Beacon Stone Row is less than 150 yards south of the Beacon, and consists of 8 stones; length 66 ft., and is 20 yards west of the old reave wall which runs south from the Beacon.

Pen Tumulus crowns the hill which is 1,404 ft. above sea level.

Pen Tumulus and Stone Row. About ⅓ mile west of the Stone Row this will be found. It consists of a Tumulus and a few stones of a Stone Row running S.W. from the Tumulus. ⅓ mile S.E. of this monument is a **Third Tumulus** which has a containing circle of 12 stones, 20 ft. in diameter.

II. 5. **Shell Top** is ¾ mile N. of Pen Beacon and is reached by a footpath trodden by cattle. Shell Tor is a very prominent cluster of rocks, really a small tor, in the south west portion of Dartmoor.

II. 6. **Yealm Valley.** The Yealm is a beautiful river, and although so short it is well worth a visit. It tumbles out of the bogs from which the Shavercombe Brook also takes its rise, coming from a great height (1,500 ft.), it proceeds in a series of cascades and enters Dendles Wood and so on. On the left bank is a ruined Blowing House, and lying about are two mould stones, one of which is within the ruins.

By following the river upward and crossing it near Yealm Rocks a clitter of granite blocks - the ruins of another Blowing House will be found, within the ruins is a mould stone

It we follow the river down we pass through Dendles Wood and back to Cornwood.

CHAPTER III.

LEE MOOR.

III. 1. **Lee Moor** though spoilt by the clay works has some very interesting remains close at hand on W. side of Crownhill Down, 1 mile South of the Lee Moor Clay Works, close to the huge clay dump. 100 yds. north of this Tumulus is a stone circle, diameter 16 ft., and seven stones remain. 150 yards S.S.W. of the Tumulus is a group of six barrows, five of which are arranged in a semicircle.

III. 2. On the east side of Collard Tor and quite near the rocky summit are **Collard Stone Rows,** about 120 ft. and 100 ft. in length respectively. One leads to a dilapidated circle, the other led up to a cairn which has been removed. Just below them now is the row of Collard Tor Cottages, which will help you find them.

III. 5. **Chambered Hut**, now in ruins, was a hut cluster with several chambers. To reach it, back to the main road near Lee Moor House, and on to the end of the wall of the enclosures attached to the cottages on the right; here take the path east which will lead you comfortably across the rough ground and the leats. At $\frac{5}{8}$ of a mile from the road the path ends, and at about 300 yards east of this point you will find the Chambered Hut in a very dilapidated condition, but at one time it was a cluster of human dwellings.

III. 6. Next back to the road to the point from which you started, **Lee Moor House** is on the right in its own grounds and is the property of Mr. Martin, who now lives at Slade, Cornwood. The rhododendrons in these groups in May and June are splendid.

III. 7. Just beyond Lee Moor House on right side of the road is **Blackaton Cross,** also called Romans Cross. The head of the cross and its base formed part of an ancient cross, but the shaft had been destroyed. The present shaft was a stone made for a window sill at Lee Moor House and was given by the late Mr. Phillips, who many years ago lived there. This public spirited man set the cross up again in its ancient base, adding the window sill for a shaft.

III. 7. **Emmets Post** is an upright stone fixed in a Tumulus. The stone is the bond stone between the lands of Sir Henry Lopes, Bart., and the Earl of Morley. From the post the path may be followed west to Shaugh Prior. This is a path used much by the workmen at the clay works as they go to and fro their work.

III. 8. The road we have just left leads on to Cadover Bridge. Follow the road on to a point where there is a short steep hill. On the moor on left is a **large pound,** containing several hut circles, the stones of the pound wall can be seen from the road.

CHAPTER IV.

CADOVER BRIDGE.

From this delightful spot many are the interests of the wayfarer. This story was told me which happened about this spot. During the Great Frost of 1855, there was a very heavy fall of snow. A Rev. Patey, Master of the Grammar School at Plympton, used to ride over to

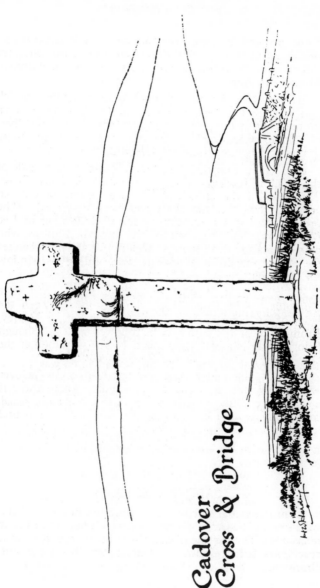

Cadover
Cross & Bridge

Drawn by MR. H. W. HARDING.

Sheepstor from Plympton, on Sundays, to take the service.
One Sunday after this fall of snow he was on the moor all
day, and never reached Sheepstor, but had to return home.
At times he had to get off and tread the snow to make it
hard enough for the pony to walk on. He was unable to
go for two or three Sundays, and when he arrived at
Sheepstor again, he was told that he was the first outsider
they had seen in the parish for three weeks. Exactly the
same thing was told to a man who came into Sheepstor
three weeks after the blizzard of 1891.

IV. 1.   To **Shaugh Prior** take road to right and then
turn right again at the first turning.

IV. 2.   **Cadover Cross** was re-erected by me in 1915.
It lay on the ground for many years near where it stands
now. I gave it a new shaft and set it up.

IV. 3.   In 1873 this cross was noticed lying down by
the soldiers encamped on Ringmoor Down, and they set
it up on the soil, but it had fallen again. When I had
fixed a new shaft to the fine head, we were wondering
where to fix it, and chose a green sward in the heather.
We were digging a hole for the shaft intending to set it in
cement, when we came across a large block of stone. This
proved to be the original socket stone *in situ*. It had this
unusual feature, the socket hole was 13 inches deep and
quite perforated the stone. So all we had to do was to fix
it in its original position—a very satisfactory restoration.

Note this cross has three small incised crosses on its
face, one on the head, and one on each of the arms—no
other Dartmoor Cross is like this.

IV. 4.   This is the country of Dewer, the wild huntsman, who with his fire-breathing hounds hunts the moor
on dark stormy nights.

> " All night long in the dark and the Wet,
> Dewer goes riding by."

IV. 5.   **Cadworthy Kistvaen.**   Follow the wall near the
cross and pass Cadworthy Farm which is below, on the
south side of the wall. Keep to the wall until it suddenly
bends towards the river, at this bend is the Kistvaen
which has its containing stone circle, but the stones are
all prostrate.

DEWER, THE WILD HUNTSMAN

From this point go on to

IV. 6. Carrington Rock, which overlooks the valley of the Plym, and the view is very fine.

Note, as you approach the rock the hill has been forti·fied, and has a stone wall round it except west and south.

The Dewerstone, a fine crag, is just below.

IV. 7. Wigford Circle is on the top of Wigford Down. It has only four stones, which are huge slabs ; the cairn which they enclosed was carted away some years ago ; 26 cart loads were taken away. Also near by are the ruins of two large cairns.

IV. 8. From the pond follow the road west towards Hooe Meavy. At ½ mile take to the moor along a gra·sy track on left side of the road. In 200 yards are the remains of a small circle, which is 40 yards in a straight line from the road. The diameter is 30 ft., but only a semi-circle is left. Only six stones remain, the largest of which is four ft. 300 yards further south west is the junction of four green paths, here is a stone circle almost complete. There are 18 stones, diameter 30 ft. This circle has been the containing circle of a large cairn, which has long ago been carted away.

Both these circles are on a raised platform, and the stones, most of them are of the slab type, laid long ways.

They have been much alike and about the same size

IV. 9. Good a-Meavy Cross. Along the road referred to about ½ mile on, you come to a place where four ways meet. Here turn left, and on to Good-a-Meavy. On the moor just outside the gate we enter to turn down to Good-a-Meavy, stands Good-a-Meavy Cross. On its site originally stood the base of an ancient cross which pointed the way to the ford below. This was taken away some years ago, and is now in the grounds of Good-a-Meavy House, and forms the base there of a memorial cross to Mr. Hill's son, who was killed at the Dardanelles during the war. Mr. Hill very generously consented to place the present cross on the green where it is, and I was present when it was completed.

IV. 10.   Below Good-a-Meavy House the Meavy flows on its way to meet the Plym at Shaugh Bridge.   It is very pretty about here ; after crossing the bridge the road leads on to Roborough Down.

IV. 11.   Back to the Four Ways and go on down to Hooe Meavy.   This was a lovely glen before the trees were cut down during the war.   Cross Hooe Meavy Bridge and pass through **Clearbrook.**

At Clearbrook the road runs south west across Roborough Down and meets the main road (Plymouth to Yelverton). As you come out on to the main road on the right hand side an ancient cross-base stood, but a few years ago it disappeared; it was fractured but that it was a cross-base is beyond dispute.   No doubt it marked the way leading to Hooe Meavy and the moor beyond.

About half-way along the road between Brisworthy Pond and Hooe Meavy is a cross-base beside the road.

CHAPTER V.

SHAUGH.

1—*Shaugh Bridge.*   2—*Plym Gorge.*   3—*The Dewerstone*
4—*Carrington Rock.*   5—*Shaugh Church.*

From the halt bearing this name some delightful rambles may be made.

V. 1.   **Shaugh Bridge,** one mile, is situated at the entrance of the gorge of the Plym, and is a favourite resort of picnic parties
The scenery here is very grand, and a walk should be taken up the gorge as far as the Dewerstone.

Old Shaugh Bridge was destroyed by a great flood on January 27th, 1823, which was caused by the sudden melting of a deep snow accompanied by a deluge of rain, a combination which causes nearly all very exceptional floods on Dartmoor.

V. 2   **Plym Gorge,** which is entered at Shaugh Bridge, is one of the most picturesque on the moor.   It is seen to best advantage either from the top of the Dewerstone or from the path above the Clay works which winds up the south side of the Gorge to Cadover Bridge. On its northern side are five distinct spurs of rock which rise out of the woods which clothe the sides of the Gorge. The finest of these is :—

V. 3. **The Dewerstone**, a magnificent precipice, whose base is lapped by the limpid waters of the Plym, and whose beetling crags are still the home of the raven. A few hundred yards up stream the Plym plunges over a bar of granite forming a small but charming cascade.

V. 4. **Carrington Rock**. This is a stiff climb from Shaugh Bridge, but one which is attempted by nearly all visitors, except the infirm and the indolent. After crossing the wooden

ONE OF THE NEW BENCH-ENDS IN
SHEEPSTOR CHURCH.
THE VINE AND THE DOVE.

bridge, a zigzag path winds up to the Rock, from which there is a magnificent view. Carrington's name and the date are cut on the face of the highest rock. The return to the bridge may be made by descending the footpath on the south side of the Rock.

A walk from the Rock to Sheepstor is described in walk (24) of my Sheepstor chapter

There are the remains of an ancient camp on this hill, above the Dewerstone.

V. 5. **Shaugh Church** (1½ miles) is a fine old moorland shrine, with an imposing tower which is a landmark for miles.

The church was struck by lightning in 1823.

Shaugh has one of the finest font covers in the county. It is made of oak and beautifully carved. Just over 30 years ago it narrowly escaped destruction.

This splendid work of art was accounted as unfit to adorn the sanctuary of God, and it was cast out of the sanctuary as a worthless and unholy thing, and placed in a barn. Providentially it was rescued and restored to the church, and it again adorns and beautifies—

> ". . . . the sacred Font,
> And there the Holy Dove
> To pour is ever wont
> His blessings from above."

Note the stone quatre-partite groined roof in the porch.

There is a base of an octagonal cross in the church-yard on the south side of the church, and a good speci-men of the Dartmoor cross is built into the vicarage hedge, and will be seen on the right as one passes up the road. This road leads out on to Shaugh Moor.

Where the road enters on the moor, about 100 yards north, beside the road is another cross. There is another cross base near the cross roads where the Wattor road meets the Plympton road.

To Shaugh Moor which is covered with antiquities of one sort and another. See Collard Stones Rows (III. 2).

On Shaugh Beacon is a curious stone which has been used as a Cromlech at some time. It is really nature's work, but there is no doubt it has formed part of a cromlech.

Shaugh Barrow.   From Shaugh Church take the road to Cadover Bridge, on reaching the open moor turn left. Soon as you approach Shaden Brake on right side of the road you will see this fine barrow.

Shaugh Circle and Stone Row.   From the barrow at a distance of 360 ft. east will be found these remains.

The circle is at the south end of the row, and has still three stones standing, and three down.   It has a diameter of 51 ft., the row points slightly east of the circle.   The stones of the row are small, but it is very perfect, except that a few stones were taken away just before I found it in 1917.

Shaugh to Trowlesworthy Circle and Stone Rows.   To Cadover Bridge, then turn to the left, and take the first turning to the left again to Trowlesworthy Warren. Trowlesworthy is a very ancient tenement, and is referred to in a deed dated 1290   After passing by the Warren House, with its curious courtyard, strike the leat 100 yards above the house.   In less than a mile, southwards, the leat passes right through the antiquities.   On its north bank is the circle of eight stones, 23 ft. in diameter ; and a very fine double stone row, 420 ft. long, which the leat cuts in two.   It runs down to the base of the hill, where it terminates in a large menhir, which has been moved a few yards away from its original position.

On the west side of the leat, opposite the circle, is another fine stone row, 250 ft. long, terminating in a blocking stone.   It formerly led up to a circle which needs restoring.   Some of its stones are under the turf. The hillside above the leat is strewn with antiquities. The old tenant at Trowlesworthy, John Lavers, died on March 15th, 192 , in the ninety-fifth year of his age. The moor was covered with a deep snow on the day of his funeral, but the March sun melted it 3 ft. in the day.

CHAPTER VI.

BRISWORTHY.

VI. 1.   At Brisworthy, outside the farm as you enter the lane to go down to Brisworthy Burrows, is a large boulder close to the gate.   Note it has 17 dents in it, this was an old mortar stone, and belonged to a Blowing House which formerly stood in the field on the other side of the stone wall, just inside the gate.

VI. 2.   When this lane comes out on the moor follow the wall westward.   In 100 yards in a corner is the site of a blowing house ; two mortar stones are there now, and some years ago Mr. R. Hansford Worth found an old furnace base stone, which alas ! has disappeared and can nowhere be found.

VI. 3.   **Brisworthy Circle.**   This is a very fine specimen of the stone circle, and is situated at the southern extremity of Ringmoor Down, where the ground slopes down to Legis Lake.

The Down probably takes its name from this ring of stones.

It is very easily found if one strikes the wall which runs from Brisworthy Plantation eastwards down to the Legis Lake.   This wall divides the moorland from the new-takes of Brisworthy Farm.

If visitors who are motoring or driving, desire to visit this interesting monument, they should drive to Brisworthy Farm and leave their conveyance there, and then take the lane which leads north-eastwards, which will soon bring them out on to the moor, and which passes close by the circle.   As they approach the moor the circle will be seen ahead.   The circle is one of the finest on Dartmoor, although the Grey Wethers and Scor Hill are larger specimens.   Its diameter is about 80 ft., and it consists of 24 stones.   All except three lay prostate on the ground until the summer of 1909, when Mr. R. Hansford Worth and I re-erected the stones of this fine monument.

Several stones are missing on the south side, which are evidently in the wall near by.

One stone on the west side, is a very curious shape, having a slight resemblance to the very curious stone in the pulpit circle near Trowlesworthy,

BRISWORTHY CIRCLE

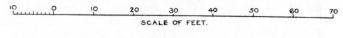

SCALE OF FEET.

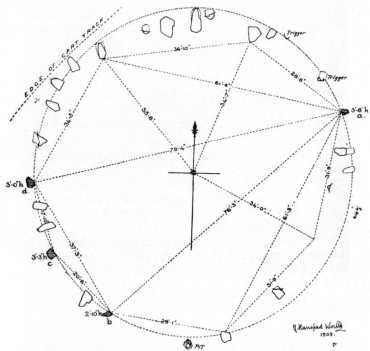

Excavations in the centre disclosed the presence of wood ashes and charcoal,

Mrs, Wheeler, at Brisworthy Farm, will provide tea for visitors,

VI. 4, **Brisworthy Tumulus** will be found 50 yards to the east of the circle, where the ground slopes down towards Legis Lake.

Little more than the site now remains, with two stones of the small enclosing circle.

Here again digging operations disclosed the presence of charcoal. There are traces of a stone row which formerly ran from the tumulus down to the lake.

LEGIS LAKE KISTVAEN.

VI. 5. **Legis Lake Kistvaen** is situated 300 yards N.N.E. of the circle.

This is a very fine and complete specimen of the kist-vaen, although not nearly so large as those at Cadworthy or at Drizzlecombe. It is very complete, and evidently has an enclosing circle, the stones of which are all down.

A stone row originally led up to it from the westward, but only a few stones of it remain now.

C

This kistvaen seems to have been unknown to the present generation, until I discovered it in the spring of 1908. To find it, get the gate in the wall and the clay heap in a line.

VI. 6. **Ringmoor Circle and Stone Row.** These remains are not difficult to find, if the following directions are followed.

After leaving the kistvaen and proceeding a few yards to the N.W., the remains of a low reeve wall will be struck, which time and weather have nearly obliterated. The grassy reeve runs westward. If this be followed about 200 yards it will be found at the top of the hill to pass right through the stone row which leads up to the circle.

$\frac{1}{2}$ m. N. *almost* in a line with the end stone is Sheepstor circle. It is quite a small circle, 23 ft. diameter, and encloses a barrow. Note, the stones on south side are the largest. 200 yards east is another small barrow.

Ringmoor circle doubtless originally enclosed a cairn, and is 42 ft. in diameter, and now consists of ten stones, only three of which were standing.

The stone row, which is a single row for some distance and then double, runs N.E. for 450 yards, and many of the stones, especially at the further end, are buried under the heather.

Nearly all the stones of this monumenet were re-erected by the Rev. S. Baring-Gould, Mr. R. Hansford Worth, and myself in August, 1911.

VI. 7. **Sites of Seven Tumuli** will be found if the track from Sheepstor circle be followed across Ringmoor Down until you approach a stone wall. If before reaching the wall you turn and set your course due N., you will find on the slope of the hill the remains of seven tumuli which have formed huge cairns at some time. If the wall be followed up, remains of an eighth tumulus is found near the wall on its west side.

VI. 8. **Gutter Tor Hut Circles.** These very fine specimens of the hut circle will be found near the wall on its east side, and to the south side of the postman's walk.

Gutter Tor Kistvaen. The remains of a small kistvaen will be seen on the west side of the wall, and about 100 yards from the wall by the hut circle Alas, only the enclosing stones remain.

Gutter Tor Rock Basin will be found on the top of the southern rock of the tor. It is a very fair specimen.

VI. 9. **Nattor Tumulus** is easily found, whether approaching from Sheepstor village or from Gutter Tor.

From Sheepstor the road which runs by Colyton out on to the moor, and which passes Nattor Farm, should be followed until you get to a thorn bush standing near a gate – on the opposite side of the road is the tumulus, which has been a very large one. It has no enclosing circle of stones.

CHAPTER VII.

DITSWORTHY WARREN.

VII. 1. **Sheepstor to Ditsworthy Warren** (three miles).

A very pleasant walk from Sheepstor. Follow the lane beyond Sheepstor Church past Colyton. Just above the farm you pass through a gateway on to the moor. Then *either* keep straight on to Burracombe Gate, and then take the track to the right, which will lead you to the Warren House, which is just below the low tor ahead.

At the gate above Colyton, which I have mentioned, take the footpath on the moor which runs parallel with the road for some distance and then passes directly over Gutter Tor. At the top of the tor the path will be seen below, winding its way to the Warren House.

Or still another way. At the gate above Colyton take the footpath across the top of Ringmoor to Ringmoor Gate. Here you join the road to the Warren, which should be followed.

3, 4, 17.   3, 16.   3, 15.

VII. 2. **To Drizzlecombe Antiquities** (four miles). At the back of the Warren House is a track which passes right by the remains on its way to Plym Steps. (The track which turns off to the left leads to Eylesbarrow).

Along the track you presently come to a ruined kistvaen. Here you can begin your explorations. A rough plan of the remains is given on my plan of antiquities.

They consist of three stone rows leading to cairns, enclosed in stone circles. Each row ends in a menhir, which forms the blocking stone. View the Great Menhir, which is 18 ft. high from all sides. On the north side it has a most weird

DRIZZLECOMBE MENHIR AND ROW.

appearance. In this wild and desolate country this great menhir has for thousands of years kept its lonely watch over its honoured dead. The foot of man seldom passes by, but—

> " At noon the wild bee hummeth
> About the mossed headstone ;
> At midnight the moon cometh,
> And looketh down alone."

Near by is the Giant's Grave, the largest cairn on the moor. 290 yards north of the cairn is the large kistvaen

on a low mound.   At the north west foot of the cairn is
a tiny kistvaen.

The whole of this desolate country is strewn with the
monuments of the dead, for this was the great cemetery
of the town which covered a good portion of the hill to
the north west, in the direction of Burracombe Gate.

In retracing our steps towards Sheepstor, if we examine
this hill we shall find the ruins of huts in all directions.

DITSWORTHY WARREN.

Many of the huts seem to have been so deep, a feature
which suggests that the prehistoric men who lived here
possessed the luxury of capacious wine cellars.

The easiest way back to Sheepstor is to proceed N.N.W.
from Drizzlecombe and to strike the rough road from
Eylesbarrow.

3, 16, 19.   4, 3.

VII. 3.   **To Plym Steps** (six miles).   Route same as VII.
2 as far as the Giant's Grave.   From this point follow

Photo by] DRIZZLECOMBE MENHIR. [Mr. R. C. Letheren.

the path right up the Plym Valley. The stream which meets the Plym where the river bends is the Langcombe. Just above are Plym Steps. On the bank of the river is an old blowing house.

Just before reaching the Langcombe, you see on your left hand a fine pound and a cairn on its S.W. side.

Follow the Plym up till you come to the Abbot's Ford.

DITSWORTHY WARREN KITCHEN.

The most direct way to Plym Steps is to take the track from Burracombe Gate to Eylesbarrow Mine Ruin, $\frac{1}{2}$ mile before reaching the ruin take the cart track which turns right. The cart track ascends the rising ground beyond the stream and leads across the moor to Plym Steps and the Langcombe Valley. The tors passed on the left are Higher and Lower Harter Tors.

VII. 4. **To Deadman's Bottom and Grim's Grave at Langcombe Head** (six miles.) Route same as VII. 3 to the point where the Langcombe joins the Plym. Here cross the Plym and ascend the hill. On the top of the hill, a little to the left, will be found Plym Steps Kistvaen, surrounded by a nice circle of stones, which are all down. The tor to the north is Calveslake Tor. On its eastern slopes is another kistvaen.

Continuing one's walk eastward, you soon come to Deadman's Bottom. Here, well above the river, on your left will be found an interesting group of remains—two fine kistvaens in ruins and two circles which were used as crematoria.

In the little rill, which comes from the marshy ground above in Deadman's Bottom, are most exquisite mosses of all shades and colours, the prettiest I have ever seen.

Continuing one's walk to the head of the Langcombe, Grim's Grave lies close to the stream. It is a very fine kistvaen, second only to Lakehead Kistvaen near Postbridge; but the kistvaen at Deadman's Bottom will be still finer if carefully restored, as the capstone is so very large.

In dry weather, by striking N.E. from Grim's Grave, you can reach Broad Rock, but it is marshy ground, as it is near the head of the Erme.

VII. 5. **To Shavercombe and Hen Tor** (four miles). Start at Ditsworthy Bridge, which is just below the Warren House. After crossing the bridge, take the track to the left, which will bring you to Shavercombe, which is the next dip in the hills. Here is a sweet little dell, such as one would least expect to find in such a desolate part of the moor.

In the little gorge is a waterfall, which is very fine after rain (See Frontispiece). 150 yards S.S W. of the waterfall is a fine kistvaen, and nearly 300 yards S.E. of this monument are the ruins of another.

Here strike across the moor for Hen Tor, which is a fine pile of rocks. Ascend the tor from its east side, which is quite easy.

On the top of the tor, facing west, is a recess, where one can lie full length and bask in the sun, quite sheltered from a cold east wind.

On descending from the tor, you can make your way

back to Ditsworthy Bridge through the ruins of Hen Tor Farm, which has been tenantless for more than a hundred years.

The old saying, "Drive the natural away and it returns at a gallop," is well illustrated on the slopes of Hen Tor, where formerly there was Hen Tor Farm, which was abandoned a century ago. Nature has so rapidly resumed her sway that most of the traces of the farm have disappeared.

VII. 6. **To Ditsworthy Circle, Willing's Wall Circle and Kistvaen** (4 miles). After crossing Ditsworthy Bridge, bear to the right. You soon come to the Hen Tor Brook. Just before you reach it you will come upon a very interesting hut circle. It has a protecting wall on its S.W. side, built to protect its prehistoric tenants from the bad weather.

Next proceed S.E. towards Willing's Wall. About 200 yards on the north side of the wall, and not far from the east bank of Hen Tor Brook, you will find Ditsworthy Circle, which formerly enclosed two kistvaens, the cover stones of which are still among the ruins. The circle consists of 16 stones and is about 23 ft. in diameter, and is very dilapidated, and much hidden by the heather.

Next strike Willing's Wall, and then follow it in the westerly direction. It soon crosses the Hen Tor Brook. About 100 yards from the brook, near the north side of the wall, is a good specimen of the kistvaen.

Continuing one's walk to the top of the hill, about half way between Hen Tor Brook and Spanish Lake, Willing's Wall Circle will be found. It consists of six clusters of three or four stones in each cluster, erected at intervals. Some of the stones are down. The diameter of the circle is about 140 ft. The wall has been built into the southern arc of the circle, and has taken some of its stones.

VII. 7. **To Spanish Lake, Shell Top, Pen Beacon and Cornwood.** Cross the Plym by the stones where it is joined by Spanish Lake. Ascend the little dell formed by Spanish Lake ; near the head of the dell turn left up the hill. As there is a considerable swamp at the head of

Spanish Lake, which also covers a good deal of ground towards Shell Top, it will be necessary to keep up well on the high ground. When Shell Top, which is a small tor, comes into view, get to the head of the swamp and then strike out for Shell Top ; thence is only a short mile on to Pen Beacon, from which a low reeve wall runs to Shell Top. Along its east side runs a little path—a sheep track. If this be followed, Pen Beacon is easily ascended. On the west side of the beacon, a few yards away, is a fine hut circle. From the beacon descend into Cornwood across the slopes of Cornwood Common. (See II. 4).

From Shell Top, Hen Tor is only 1 mile about due north. The ground between the two tors is rather rough.

From Spanish Lake, Great and Little Trowlesworthy Tors are easily ascended. There is a ruined wall on the north slope of Great Trowlesworthy Tor called " Irishmen's Wall."

CHAPTER VIII.

SHEEPSTOR.

SHEEPSTOR VILLAGE.

NOWHERE on Dartmoor is there a place so beautiful and
fair as the quaint and picturesque little village of Sheepstor. Nestling under the great tor from which it takes its
name, it is well sheltered from the mountain winds.
    From the brow of Yennadon—

" Deep lies the valley, girt with rock and wood,
In rural wise the scattered hamlet stood,—
Lake, crag, cascade adorn the scene,
Gardens and fields and shepherds' walks between,
Through all, a streamlet, from its mountain source
Seen but by stealth, pursues its rocky course."

This old-world hamlet was famed in years gone by for its exceedingly pretty country dances and its clever old fiddler, William Andrew, who knew all the dance tunes.

THE SUNDIAL, SHEEPSTOR.

The dear old fiddler has gone to his rest years ago, but the old country dances are still preserved, and may be seen at the Harvest Festivals.

" Sheepstor is the most truly rural parish in Devonshire." These were the words used a few days ago by a diocesan official who knows every corner of Devonshire

to convey to me the impression Sheepstor always gives
him.

Sheepstor is one of the few parishes still in Venville.
In return for a fine we pay to the Duchy, we have certain
rights. On the Duchy lands we can pasture ponies and
cattle, cut peat for our fires, and take away anything from
the moor which may do us good, except green oak and
venison. As the oak tree does not grow on the Duchy
lands in this neighbourhood, and the deer is extinct on
Dartmoor, there is no fear of our rights being exceeded.

The Venville rights originated many hundreds of years
ago. Several of the explanations of their origin which I
have seen are incorrect. They were originally granted to
the farmers in return for the services they rendered to the
Forester in assisting him in exterminating the wolves
which infested the forest long after they were extinct in
other parts of England. As evidence that wolves infested
English forests later than is generally supposed, there is
an interesting tomb of a Bishop of Wells in Wells
Cathedral, dated about 1200, on which are recorded the
noble deeds of the prelate. One of his exploits recorded
was the material assistance which he rendered in exterminating the wolves in the great forest of Mendip by
hunting.

VIII. 1. **The Village Cross.** As we enter the old church
town, with its truly rural surroundings, the first object
that arrests our attention is the ancient cross, standing
on a rugged but very substantial base. In 1910, the cross
was restored to its rightful place in the middle of the
parish. For a great number of years it has been used as
a rubbing-post for cattle, and previous to that as a gate-
post. We recently gave it new arms, and the men of
Sheepstor combined and built the large base and re-
erected the cross as a memorial of the Coronation of H.M.
King George V. The men nobly devoted their evenings
to the work for three weeks without any remuneration.

This is the fine old spirit of self-sacrifice and self-
devotion, which has been the means of building many of
our fine country churches centuries ago.

We hope the old cross may stand on Sheepstor Green for many centuries to come, as a witness to their work and labour of love.

In shape there is no other on the moor quite like it, while the cross in relief on both sides is not found on any other Dartmoor cross.

The cross is seen very well outside the church porch, and whenever a coffin rests on the coffin stone of the lych gate, the cross, being in a line, stands immediately above it. This is a very impressive feature, and quite un-designed. It was dedicated by the vicar on the afternoon of Coronation Day—June 22nd, 1911—in order that it may be used as a preaching cross, and open-air services held there.

The Fine War Memorial Cross which stands opposite the Church door was erected in memory of William Mortimore and Harry Blatchford who gave their lives for their country.

VIII. 2. **The Lych Gate** is a very fine specimen. Its crumbling oak beams testify to its great age.

A small pedestal for a saint will be noticed on the wall of the house outside the lych gate.

VIII. 3. **The Church.** The church is a typical Dart-moor church in the perpendicular style. Its large square embattled tower has turrets at each corner with fine crocketted pinnacles.

The tower contains a peal of six bells, five of which were cast in 1769. One bears the inscription, " I call the quick to church and the dead to grave." Through the very praiseworthy efforts of my predecessor, the Rev. H. Leigh Murray, the five bells were re-hung and a sixth added in 1904, and now there is a beautiful peal.

The weather-beaten tower is of great beauty, and the turrets and pinnacles yellow with a beautiful lichen. Here

> " Alone, and warming his five wits,
> The white owl in the belfry sits."

In the north wall is a monument to the sister-in-law of Sir Francis Drake, and another to the memory of one of the Elfords.

The organ was completely renovated in 1909 at a cost of over £100.

A fine octagonal cross, recently repaired, is fixed in the stile to the south of the church porch. The shaft has been there a great number of years. The cross stands

COPYRIGHT.   SHEEPSTOR CHURCH.

THE BULL RING.

seven feet above the level of the ground, and was formerly much taller. I found another piece of the shaft in the wall at the side of the stile, but it was broken. The broken piece is now in the corner of the base of the Village Cross.

There are the remains of a very curious sundial over the church porch, which bears the initials of John Elford, of Longstone, and is dated 1640. It also has the following inscriptions :—" Et hora sic vita " ; " Mors janua vitae." It consists of a skull and cross-bones, resting on an hour-glass, with ears of corn sprouting from the eye sockets. It is symbolical of " life out of death."

The Rood Screen was completed at Easter, 1914, at a cost of £450, and was dedicated on May 13th by the Lord Bishop of Exeter. One door and other fragments of the original fifteenth century screen are incorporated in the new Screen. This magnificent Screen consists of nine bays with beautiful tracery, and is 28 ft. long. The vaulting is exquisitely done. The panels of the vaulting and also the cornice is adorned with very elaborate car-

Crazywell or Classenwell Pool, near Sheepstor.

vings; and the same enrichment, but with a different pattern, will be found on the east side of the chancel portion.

The Screen was brought to Sheepstor on March 3rd and 4th, 1914, by road across Dartmoor from Exeter. God arrayed Dartmoor in white garments to receive the Screen. On both days the moor was covered with deep snow. A month's hard work fixed the screen in its position in the Church.

VIII. 4. **The Well of St. Leonard** is by the roadside opposite the house to the east of the churchyard. This is a very ancient well, and is described in deeds belonging to the parish of the reign of Queen Elizabeth. It was restored in 1910. The waters of many of the Cornish wells were highly valued for their healing properties. In many parishes the water from the Holy Well was always used in the administration of the Sacrament of Holy Baptism   There are no records to show that any value was attached in bygone days to the waters of the Well of St. Leonard, but it is a very ancient and interesting spring.

VIII. 5. **The Bull Ring** was found in August, 1908, in the middle of the Vicarage field, on the south side of the church, embedded eighteen inches below the soil.   Its existence under the turf was discovered by Mr. Amos Shillibeer, who told us that he was ploughing the field one day more than forty years ago, and the point of his plough share caught in the ring and pulled him up very abruptly. We made a prolonged search with crowbars, and eventually his son, Mr. George Shillibeer, came upon it.

It is now raised to the level of the ground, and can easily be seen from the churchyard ; and the large granite block to which it is fixed, which is five feet long, is placed in exactly the same position as that in which it was found.

The Bull Ring was formerly used for bull-baiting. The bull was tied to the ring and then baited with dogs. The dogs, which were killed in the fray, were usually buried under the stone which supported the ring.

At these barbarous festivities the women wore peculiar aprons, in which they caught the bull-dog when it was tossed.   The villagers irreverently held their feastings and festivities amongst the tombstones in the churchyard. While a fight was going on, the spectators sat along the churchyard wall and watched the fun, repairing at frequent intervals to the ale-house adjoining the field for refreshment   The old sport has long since died out, but the old ale-house still continued to refresh the thirsty within the memory of some people still living.   Some years ago it was pulled down, with the cottage adjoining, and the building now seen is St. Leonard's Room.

Although bull-baiting was indulged in at Sheepstor in the days of long ago, there is no evidence whatever to support the statement that I have heard made, that prize-fighting was prevalent there.

The Old Vicarage, or Priest's House, adjoins the church-yard, and was built about 1300 and restored in 1658. The date carved in relief on the wall records the restoration.

The Church House, on the south side of the church-yard, is now the Parish Room.

VIII. 6. **The Rajah's Tomb** is under the large beech tree in the churchyard. It is the Mecca of West Country tourists, who go and stare at the tomb without having the least notion of the history of the hero whose memory it perpetuates. Some go so far astray as to think that the famous Rajah was a black man. (See "Rajah Brooke.")

Pixies

Sheepstor itself is traditionally held to be rich in precious metals carefully guarded by pixies, who it would appear are sufficiently niggardly in their habits.

> Little pixy, fair and slim,
> Without a rag to cover him.

The miner hears the tinkle of the pixy hammers in the depths of the mine, but the pixy never offers him any of the golden ore he has extracted. A pixy who visited nightly a farmhouse near Sheepstor, and swept the hearth and did various kind offices for the house, for which he was repaid by a cake left out for him each night, was pitied by the farmer's wife, who peered at him through a chink, because he was so ragged and torn in his apparel, so—in the kindness of her heart—she made him a little suit of broadcloth and laid it in the kitchen for him. When the pixy saw this, away went his tatters, and arraying himself in the new suit he capered about, singing

> Pixy fine and pixy gay,
> Pixy now will run away.

One notion anciently held on the moor, was that the souls of unbaptised babies that had died passed wailing in the wind.

The wind blows cold on waste and wold,
　　It bloweth night and day ;
The souls go by 'twixt earth and sky,
　　Impatient, cannot stay.
They fly in clouds and flap their shrouds,
　　When full the moon doth sail,
In dead of night, when lacketh light,
　　We hear them pipe and wail.

And many a soul with des'late howl,
　　Doth rattle at the door,
Or rove and rout. with dance and shout,
　　Around the granite tor.
We hear a soul 'i th' chimney growl,
　　That's drenched with the rain,
To wring the wet from winding sheet,
　　And see the fire 'l were fain.

But all this belongs to the past. It is doubtful whether the present generation has heard these stories. If they have they have scouted them as old wives' fables. And yet one hardly knows whether there may not linger on, though unacknowledged, some superstitious ideas imbibed in childhood. I knew a case that occurred not so many years ago when a young carpenter sat up on St. Mark's eve in the church porch. On that eve a watcher there is supposed to see pass by him the forms of those who will die in the parish in the ensuing twelve months. The young man averred most solemnly that he had seen himself pass by into the church. He took to his bed and died. The parson who visited him did his utmost to disabuse him of the idea, told him that a passing light had cast his shadow against the wall. The young carpenter would not be shaken in his conviction, and died, though there was actually nothing but sheer fright to account for his death.

Witchcraft is by no means extinct, nor faith in it, and it is to be feared that it will be a long time before the white witch ceases to be a recipient of money, and a dealer in charms. Here is a remedy which a white witch gave for a sprain :

　　　　2 ozs. of oil of turpentine
　　　　2　,,　　　,,　　earthworms
　　　　2　,,　　　,,　　swillowes (what this is I do
　　　　　　　　　　　　　not know)
　　　　2　,,　　　,,　　opedildoc

The opedildoc and the turpentine were the sole useful condiments in the composition. But usually the white witch uses verbal charms.

Of course ghosts will hold their own quite as long as the white witch. I am not aware whether any one of the old Elford's " walks " among the ruins of Longstone.

CHAPTER IX.

WALKS AROUND SHEEPSTOR.

1—*Sheep's Tor.* 2—*Round the Tor.* 3—*Nosworthy Bridge* 4—*Crazywell Pool.* 5—*Leather Tor and Peak Hill.* 6— *Nosworthy Bridge and Nillacombe Valley.* 7—*Down Tor.* 8—*Deancombe Valley.* 9—*Eylesbarrow, Nun's Cross to Princetown.* 10—*Broad Rock.*

IX. 1. **Ascent of Sheepstor** (1 mile.) The first effort every visitor with a fairly strong pair of legs sets his mind on is a scramble to the top of Sheep's Tor.

We will therefore start from Sheepstor Cross, and passing through the churchyard proceed up the lane.

Before we leave the church behind us, I should like to mention that Sheepstor Church was the scene of the goose story. Until it was separated from Bickleigh, and endowed by the late Sir Massey Lopes, Sheepstor was only entitled to one service in three weeks. One Sunday morning the Vicar of Bickleigh entered the church to conduct Divine Service, but was entreated by the clerk not to use the pulpit, as his old goose had been sitting a fortnight, and would hatch out before his next visit.

Passing up the lane, a cottage is seen on the left hand, beside the plantation. A farmhouse formerly stood here which had a history.

A thrifty farmer once lived there and saved his money, but in those days there were not the banking facilities there are to-day. One night the house was entered by robbers, who stole £200. They were traced to Plymouth and their house was searched, but no trace of the money could be found. As the police were leaving the house, they noticed a loaf on the table. They lifted it up. The crust came off, and inside were one hundred sovereigns. One robber was caught and hanged.

Continuing this walk, we are soon out on the open moor.

The name of the tor has no reference to sheep, although flocks of sheep often browse on its breezy slopes, but means " steep." The old names of the tor are Shittes Tor and Schittes Tor.

Sheep's Tor is in the midst of a fine hunting country, and is often drawn by the Dartmoor hounds. The dear old tor ne'er looks prettier than it does in the late autumn and early winter, when the hounds with the huntsmen in their scarlet coats sweep across its rocky shoulder, when the whole hillside is redder than a fox with the dead bracken.

Now for the ascent. There are several good ways. The ascent on the **north** side is very rough ; on the **west,** stiff but pleasant ; at the **southern** extremity, none but the foolhardy, would attempt to scale the precipitous rocks. On the east side is a gentle slope, very easily ascended even by the aged and infirm. To ascend the *west* side, one way is to go through Sheepstor, following the road up to the tor until you pass through the gate just beyond the iron cottage. A few yards further on, branch off across the moor from the wall and follow a rough path, which is not very distinct, towards a thorn tree. Another way is to take the green lane which branches off the road opposite Park Inn. After passing through a gate at the end of the lane, a path leads you up to the tor.

The best way to ascend the *east* side is to follow route 14 to the bend of the wall, then proceed eastwards parallel with the wall one hundred yards, then turn round and ascend.

When, breathless, you reach the top, what a panorama lies before you—

> " Where the mountain's spacious breast
> Opens in airy grandeur to the West,"

where the long and rugged lines of the Cornish mountains

form the horizon.   Brown Willy, with its five peaks, can
easily be picked out.

The summit of the tor is very extensive.

> " Here at deep midnight by the moon's chill glance,
>   Unearthly forms prolong their viewless dance."

Sheep's Tor is the home of the pixies.   On the S.W.
side, among the clitters near a white rock, is the Pixies'
Cave.   Here one of the Elford's found refuge when he

Granite Bases of Cheese & Cider Presses

among Longstone ruins. Sheepstor.

From a drawing   *by Mr. H. W. Harding*

fled from Longstone during the Civil Wars.   On the
rocks at the southern end of the tor are rock basins, which,
however, have been worn through and no longer retain
water.   *3, 14, or 7, 14.

IX. 2 **Round Sheepstor** (4 miles).   Turn up the lane
facing the inn.   After passing through the gate at the end
of the lane, turn to the left.   This path will lead you to
the back of the tor, where the scenery is very fine.   After

passing through a third gate on to the moor again as you aacend the hill, pass by the rain guage (enclosed in the iron railings). Keep straight on till you come to a wall. Here you come into the track again which will lead you back to Sheepstor.

7, 7A, 7B, 14A, 31, 14.*

IX. 3. Sheepstor to Nosworthy Bridge. (2 miles).

There is a very beautiful walk beside Burrator Lake up Longstone Lane. Half a-mile down the lane you come to

*The numbers at the foot of the paragraphs refer to those on the Map in the end of the book.

the ruins of the fine old manor house of Longstone. The name indicates that a Long Stone, or Menhir, once stood near by. As the ruins are approached, notice a large gate socket in a granite post on your right hand. On the north end of the ruins lie a cheese press, a cider press, and an old crazing mill which ground the corn for the

Granite Corn Crazer

LONGSTONE MANOR
SHEEPSTOR

household. In the middle of the field, on the north side
of the house, will be noticed a granite platform. This was
the old windstrew, or threshing floor, belonging to the
manor house. I don't know of another windstrew in
England.

THE WINDSTREW, SHEEPSTOR.

Longstone House has had a great history, and was for
generations the seat of the Elford's, who were a powerful
family in the sixteenth and seventeenth centuries.

Continuing one's walk along the lane, where the hedge
comes to an end, some old millstones may be seen inside
the wire fence on the left. These were taken from Sir
Francis Drake's old mill, which formerly stood near by,
before the Reservoir was formed.

Continuing one's walk, the head of the Reservoir is
soon reached. Then follow the new road. This will

bring you to Nosworthy Bridge, one of the beauty spots of Dartmoor. Some little distance along the road, which runs between wire fences, the view of Leather Tor is very fine, and reminds one very much of the Matter horn from Zermatt, without its snows.

You can return to Dousland Station by Lowery.

7, 8A, 21A, 21, 40.

IX. 4. Sheepstor to Crazywell Pool (3½ miles).

Route same as (3) to Nosworthy Bridge; but just before reaching the bridge, turn up a footpath to the right, through the ruins of Nosworthy Farm. The path leads you to the road above Kingset. Among the trees North of these ruins, by the river side, lie several fine slag pounding hollows used by the tinners (about 17 hollows). When you reach the road above Kingset Farm, keep on till you come to a gate which leads you out on to the moor, then keep straight on along the track, passing by a gate on your right below. Keep on this rough track about 300 yards, till you come upon a little stream which runs across the road. This stream comes out of the pool.

Turn up to the left and follow the stream between its steep banks – quite a little gorge. As you approach the pool, a high bank faces you, through which the stream filters. Now cross this bank, and you find yourself at the brink of the pool.

So many people experience difficulty in finding it, but if these directions are followed it will be easily found.

The pool is one of the nine wonders of Dartmoor. In the middle is an old mine shaft, which is of great depth, and the bottom has never been fathomed. In 1844 the Devonport municipal authorities were perplexed by a shortage of their water supply, through a prolonged drought. Relying on the fathomless depth of the pool, they set to work to pump the water out and supply the town. The pool was drained, but not the shaft, and just at the critical moment someone claimed the owner- ship of the water, and the work ceased and the weird old pool was allowed to retain its secret, and is likely to do so for many a year to come.

It is said that voices are heard at the pool, calling by

name the next person who would die in the parish. The sounds are caused by the wind as it swirls over the water.

About 30 yards N. of the pool are the remains of a stone circle, and 100 yards N.E. is a ford by which the Devonport leat may be crossed,

You can return to Dousland by Leather Tor Bridge and Lowery.

7, 8, 8B, 21C. 21B, 21A, 21, 40.

IX. 5. Ascent of Leather Tor and Peak Hill (3 miles).

Follow Longstone Lane as far as the head of the Reservoir. Here follow the new road to Vineylake. Leave the farm on your right, pass it on its North side, and cross the road, and begin the ascent. Ascend about half-way between the two tors, after the wall on your left ends. Visit the Peak Hill antiquities and return to Dousland by the Princetown road.

7, 8C. 40.

IX. 6. Sheepstor to Nosworthy Bridge and Nillacombe Valley.

Follow Longstone Lane, and keep to the road which bears to the L., this will bring you to Nosworthy Bridge. The Nillacombe Valley may be ascended by a rough path which turns off to the L. as you enter the road to Deancombe. This valley is the roughest of the rough The hand of man and the forces of nature have combined to throw the valley into confusion. Its whole length is strewn with stream works. Above Kingset the Nillacombe flows through a small but wild gorge, strewn with boulders, and the heaps and pits left by the tinners. Beyond the head of the valley, Siward's Cross is quite near.

IX. 7. Sheepstor to Down Tor Stone Circle and Stone Row (4 m.)

Follow Langstone Lane nearly to Nosworthy Bridge, then turn sharply to the right. Pass the ruins of Middleworth Farm, up to Deancombe Farm ruin. From thence there are two ways. From Deancombe Farm follow up the green lane on the west side of the farm which leads up to Down Tor. You soon find yourself on the moor. Follow the wall till it takes a sharp turn to the right, then strike south-east, and in about fifty yards you come upon a cart track which leads you right by the remains

The other way, which I always think is by far the pleasanter, is by Combeshead Farm. If this latter be taken, the Stone Row and Circle show to much greater advantage, when they come into view. The following directions will make the way clear. Just before reaching Deancombe

DOWN TOR CIRCLE AND STONE ROW.

Farm, turn down the lane to the right and cross the Dean, and then take the path up the valley to Combeshead Farm. Or you can go through Deancombe Farm and take the footpath up to Combeshead Farm. On reaching the farm, pass through a gate below the farm. You then soon find yourself on an old cart track.

Follow this track across the shoulder of the tor, to a wall. You will see a gate in the wall. After passing through the gate, the Stone Row and Circle stand up against the skyline—a noble monument.

The stones were tampered with in 1880, but the late Rev. S. Baring-Gould and the late Mr Robert Burnard came to the rescue and saved this beautiful monument from destruction, in the same way as they have saved so many.

A MOORMAN's FUNERAL—of William Pengelly, aged 90—of Combeshead, in 1932.

They repaired the damage done and re-erected the fallen stones.

The Circle, which is 42 ft. in diameter, and contains 24 stones, and formerly enclosed a large kistvaen. The row is 1,175 ft. long, and it continues up to the tumulus, but the stones at this end are smaller and nearly all are under the turf. Note the tumulus on the N. side of the circle.

From the tumulus at the east end of the row, Nun's Cross Farm is very accessible. Looking eastward, you see a dip in the hills ; the farm lies in a line with this dip, not more than 200 yards. on the other side.

As you approach the farm, look to the left and you see Siward's Cross standing by the hedge at the N.W. side of the new take.

From the farm you can journey on to Princetown, or back to Sheepstor *via* Eylesbarrow ; either way provides splendid moorland scenery.

On the W. side of Down Tor, about 40 yds. above the wall, is a shelter formed by a hugh projecting boulder. One may shelter here from a passing shower.

7, 8, 35 ; or 7, 8, 32, 33, 34 ; or 7, 8, 30, 34.

From Nun's Cross is a magnificient view, which is at its best when the gorse or the heather is out in bloom. In the distance, eastward are the heights above Dartmeet, and northward the fine tors below which the East and West Dart flow – a splendid background to a fine sweep of country. On a bright afternoon in August the view is hard to beat.

Nun's Cross is one of a long line of crosses which formerly stretched from Buckfastleigh Abbey to Buckland Abbey, and marked the track across the moor used by the monks. This is not the Abbot's Way, which lies further to the south. Two more of these crosses will be found within the new-take of the ruined Farm at Fox Tor. Another has been found a little to the S.E. of Nun's Cross Farm. Two more on the moor to the N.W. of Nun's Cross, above Kingset, which we re-erected.

Another stands at the wall by the roadside just above
Vinneylake Farm, and another outside the gate on the
green opposite Lowery Farm.   A base of another lies by a
gate on the N. side of the Princetown road, about a ¼ m.
E. of Dousland Station.

IX. 8. **Sheepstor to Deancombe Valley.**   One of the
most charming walks from Sheepstor is over the southern
shoulder of the tor into the Deancombe Valley.

Follow the track along the wall above Yellowmeade.
When the wall goes no further, keep straight on and strike
the wall in front.   Then follow this wall over a stream,
and keep to it till the track passes through a gate into a
grassy field with several large boulders in it.   Then
descend into the valley.   The view down the valley is
exceedingly fine.

Ascending the opposite hill—

> " Above, beneath. immensely spread,
> Valleys and hoary rocks I view."

The view from the top of Down Tor is hardly beaten
on Dartmoor.   3, 14, 41.

IX. 9. **Sheepstor to Eylesbarrow** (4 m., time 1 hour),
and Nun's Cross (7 m.) **and Princetown** (11 m.)   To Burracombe Gate (II), and then follow the track up to the mine
buildings.   Soon after passing these buildings there is a
fork in the track ; take the track to the L. and follow it
on to Nun's Cross and Princetown.   About 200 yds. N. of
the mine Buildings are two fine tumuli close together.
The view from the further one is the very finest in this
quarter of the moor.

                3, 4, 5, 6.

IX. 10. **Sheepstor to Broad Rock.**   Same as IX. 9 as far
as Eylesbarrow mine buildings.   At the fork in the track
referred to above keep straight on.   You soon come to a
dip in the hills, where are the ruins of a house.   On your
left hand is a delightful spring of water which gushes
forth from a veritable subterranean reservoir.

The pond from which it springs is of great depth,
probably an old mine shaft.   There is no purer water on
Dartmoor.   The combe below is Evil Combe.

Continuing one's walk along the cart track, you soon come on to the upper waters of the Plym, which the track crosses at Abbot's Ford, and here you are on the old Abbot's Way.   There are several great trackways across the Darmoor desert.   There is *Fur Tor Cut* which passes Fur Tor—a cattle drive used by moormen to move the cattle from one place to another.   *The Abbot's Way* connects the Abbey of Buckfastleigh with Tavistock and Buckland Abbeys.   *The Sandy Way* is a very ancient trackway which crosses the moor E. to W., which passed across Fox Tot, Down Ridge, Lowery and Dousland ; it is marked by crosses.   *The Lych Way* was a track over which the bodies of moormen who had died on the moor were carried to their burial at Lydford.

(For Plym Head from Abbot's Ford follow the river to its source).   After crossing the river, steer S.E., and about 1 m. further on you will see a pole standing up with a notice board fixed to it.   This is Broad Rock—the Cranmere of the southern quarter of the moor. All around is very boggy ground, although no danger exists for those who will use ordinary common sense.

From this high and boggy land the inhabitants of Sheepstor secure their peat for fuel, &c.

If you steer S.W. you come to Langcombe Kistvaen in the valley of that name.   Thence you can return by Ditsworthy to Sheepstor.

Or from Broad Road, Plym Head lies about 1 m. due N., but the ground is very swampy for a good part of the way.

As you approach Plym Head the ground is firm, and it is a pleasant walk down the Plym to Abbot's Ford, which is crossed to go to Broad Rock.

IX. 11. **Yellowmead Circles.**   The existence of the fine prehistoric stone monument, which the megalithic circles on Yellowmead Down, Sheepstor form, was unknown until 1921, and is the greatest discovery of recent years on Dartmoor.   The honour of the discovery rests with Mr. R. Hansford Worth, whose skilled eye noted the humps formed by the stones which were lying prostrate under

Photos by] YELLOWMEAD CIRCLES. [*Mr. R. Hansford Worth*

the turf which formed the outer circle, of which only one large stone and two small ones were standing, and he expressed the opinion that it was probably a double circle.

That they had escaped detection so long was due in some measure to the fact that they had for many years been covered with a very high growth of heather ; this was burnt a year or so before Mr. Worth made his discovery. Owing to the prolonged drought of the 1921 summer, I

Photo by]   YELLOWMEAD CIRCLES.   *[R Hansford Worth*

noticed that there were many patches of whortleberry scrubs and grass which were burnt up inside the large circle, which indicated the presence of stones buried not far under the surface.

FOUR CONCENTRIC CIRCLES.

In the autumn of 1921, on behalf of the Dartmoor Preservation Society, Mr. William Manning, of Yellowmead Farm, close by, and I, with the assistance of others, took in hand the task of unearthing these buried stones

D

and re-erecting them in their old socket holes. It proved
a formidable task, for we found instead of one circle that
there were four concentric circles.

Of these four circles the outer circle is composed of
large stones, many of them slabs about 4 ft. by 6 ft. It is
very incomplete, as some of the stones have been taken
away and built into the newtake wall of Yellowmead Farm,
about 100 yards to the west. The depressions in the
ground show that large stones have evidently been
removed from the north east arc; these have probably
been removed to form the small bridge across the streamlet
in the gully 200 yards north-west of the circle. The three
stones which form this bridge have such a strong likeness
to the other slabs which form the outer circle, that their
origin can hardly be doubted. This outer circle consists
now of 24 stones, and has a diameter of 66 ft. Some of
the small stones in the west arc may be only triggers of
much larger stones which have been taken away to build
the wall. The largest stone in the south-east arc was 5 ft.
6 in. as it lay on the ground, but is now 4 ft. 3 in. high.
It has on its top two or three depressions which have the
appearance of cup markings. It bears remarkable resemblance to the largest stone in the Brisworthy Circle; its
height is the same, and its girth near the bottom is also of
the same measurement.

The second circle consists of 28 stones, and has a
diameter of 50ft. It is composed of smaller stones, which
are placed with marked regularity on the east and south
sides.

The third circle consists of 31 small stones, and has a
diameter of 37 ft.

The fourth and innermost circle consists of 21 stones,
and has a diameter of 22 ft. It is composed of thick
ponderous stones. This enclosed either a kistvaen, of
which no trace remains, or a large cairn, of which there
are still indications. It encircled the burial-place of some
king or powerful chief of pre-historic times. The Dartmoor Preservation Society intends to excavate this inner
platform in the hope of finding an urn.

These four concentric circles are, therefore, composed of no less than 104 stones, and the whole monument consists of 118 stones.

THE OUTSTANDING STONES.

On the west side are 14 stones, which have formed the beginnings of probably as many as eight or nine stone rows running parallel in a westerly direction. These have all been destroyed to build the newtake wall, although on the way they are still traceable. The largest of these stones close ro the circle is trigged up by a large natural boulder which is buried underground. About 161 ft. east of the circle are the remains of a small barrow which has been contained by a small circle of stones. four of which remain, and which has a diameter of 10 ft.

About 80 yards further east is a large slab about $5\frac{1}{2}$ ft. square Connected with it are two or three stones which have formerly stood erect. About 130 yards north east of the circles is a fallen mennir, 6 ft. 3 in. long; connected with it are three stones running in a south-easterly direction.

HOW TO REACH THE CIRCLES.

After passing through Sheepstor turn to the left and go up the lane towards the tor. After passing through the gate on to the open moor follow the road until you come to another gate. Enter this and follow the green lane until you come to the open moor again ; here turn to the right towards the fir trees; the circles are on the east side of these. As you cross the gully on to the open moor, the three stones spanning the streamlet of which I have spoken will be crossed.

The leat course which runs along the west side of the circles discharged itself into the gully about 50 yards above this bridge for the purpose of turning the water wheel of a blowing house which formerly stood there, and of which, now not a single trace remains except the leat.

CHAPTER X.
DOUSLAND.

1—*Sheepstor.* 2—*Meavy.* 3—*Vixen Tor and Merrivale Bridge.* 4—*Peak Hill Antiquities.* 5—*Lowery Tor, Sharpitor and Leather Tor.* 6—*Black Tor.* 7—*Leat Falls.* 8—*Nosworthy Bridge* 9—*Round Leather Tor.* 10—*Classenwell Pool.* 11—*Brisworthy Circle.*

Photo by]　　　　　　　　　*[Mr. R. Hansford Worth.*
TIN MOULD AT COLYTON, SHEEPSTOR.

For all who desire a place conveniently situated, where they may enjoy the bracing moorland air, and at the same time have a very convenient centre for excursions, Yelverton and Dousland offer unrivalled facilities.

When staying on the moor it is a great advantage to be near a railway station, and Yelverton and Dousland each has one in its midst. Yelverton and Dousland as centres for Dartmoor excursions are second to none. If one's excursions are carefully planned, one can visit every place of interest in the western and southern portions of the moor.

The following excursions will be much appreciated by all who love the beauties of nature, whose kindly hand has lavished her gifts and her charms on Dartmoor.

MEAVY.

X. 1. **Dousland to Sheepstor** (2 m.) A very pleasant walk. After leaving the station, turn to the R. and cross the railway. In less than $\frac{1}{4}$ m. you reach Prowse's Crossing. At this point two routes are open to you. Either keep straight on and take the first turning to the L., or turn up to the L., cross the railway, and take the path across the down, which branches off in a southerly direction. Either way is extremely beautiful, and will lead you to Burrator Bridge. The waterfall at the bridge is very grand after much rain.

For Sheepstor cross the bridge.

Go one way and return the other.   Or on your return to the bridge from Sheepstor, you can turn to the R. and return to Dousland by the old lane past the plantation.

1, 1A, 2. | 2, 1. | 2, 21, 40.

X. 2. Dousland to Meavy (1 m.) Start in the same way as walk X. 1. but turn neither to the right hand nor to the left until you descend the hill. At this point in the road turn to the R. Meavy is in the valley.

A prettier village green you never saw, with its stately cross, its old-world village inn, and its venerable church in the background.

> " And in the midst an oak whose woven boughs display
> A verdant canopy of light and shade ;
> Throned on a rock its giant form appears,
> In the full manhood of eight hundred years."

SAMPFORD SPINEY CHURCH.

Under its shade in " ye olden days " the old fiddler sat and fiddled the pretty tunes of the old country dances, while the villagers danced on the green.

1, 38, 39.

The church has a fine reredos, and a curious capital in the chancel arch, which is Norman. It also has some good stained glass and a beautifully mellow peal of six bells. It formerly possessed a fine screen, but this was destroyed in 1840, and the church despoiled of much that was beautiful. The only indication now of a screen is the rood loft door behind the pulpit. There is a good waggon roof with excellent bosses.

There is a pretty walk to Sheepstor from Meavy by the side of the leat through the wood. For this, turn into the field beside the blacksmith's shop opposite the School. On the school is a replica of Drake's Drum which summons the children to school daily.

The Village Cross. This fine octagonal cross was re-placed in its present position by the Rev, W. A. G. Gray, rector for many years. He found the shaft buried up in the churchyard wall; it was set up again on August 24th, 1893, by the rector, Mr. Gray, who was assisted in the work by Fred Creber, Jack Bickle and Richard Bickle.

X. 3. **Dousland to Vixen Tor and Merrivale Bridge.** (5 m.) After leaving the station, turn to the L. and pass through Walkhampton to Huckworthy Bridge, which is very picturesque.

Huckworthy Hill is very steep. Soon after reaching the top, you will come to cross roads. Then turn to the R. and keep on this road, passing Sampford Spiney Church.

After passing through a gate, you are on the moor again, with Pew Tor in front of you. It is the road to the R. you are wanting. After passing through another gate, you enter the Vale of the Walkham. The drive up this valley in May, when the larches are putting on their spring garments and the hillsides are gorgeously apparelled with the furze bloom, is exquisitely beautiful. About a mile further on, Vixen Tor is reached; an ideal place for a picnic.

It is a short mile from here to Merrivale Bridge. About 100 yards north of the Tor is a kistvaen. First you come to a standing stone, which has been connected with it. Get the trees in the wall in a line with this stone and you will pass right by the kistvaen, which has its cover stone and a containing circle of stones. It was discovered by Dr. A. E. H. Tutton, on August 1st, 1916.

The view from the field to S.W. of the tor, looking E. over the cottage, with the hill in the background golden with furze bloom, is superb.

41, 42, 43, 44, 45, 46, 47.

There is no road between Vixen Tor and Merrivale Bridge, but the pedestrian has two alternate routes by which he can return.

Either turn down the road on the R. after crossing Merrivale Bridge. 50, 49, 48, 42, 41.

Or, by following the Tavistock road, and turning to the L. at the Moor Shop, where a fine octagonal cross with one arm will be seen, which I found in March, 1909.

60, 54, 53, 51, 43, 42, 41.

Visitors to Vixen Tor, please don't strew the ground with paper and broken bottles, which gives great annoyance to the owner.

X. 4. Dousland to Peak Hill Circle and Stone Rows.

Follow the Princetown road to the pond at the top of the hill.

The stone row, which starts from a cairn, passes through the south end of the pond, and terminates some distance below in a small circle of seven stones. About 320 yds. due east of the circle, and only 40 yds. from the road, is another stone row which has been mutilated. It is only about 30 yds. long, and starts from a ruined circle.

X. 5. Dousland to Lowery Tor, Sharpitor and Leather Tor.

Take the Princetown road, and after passing through the railway arch *above* the plantation on the R. take to the moor and ascend Peak Hill. Lowery Tor is the highest point of Peak Hill, and from it an excellent view of the Meavy Valley and Burrator Lake is obtained. Near the tor, on its W. side, is a large dilapidated cairn.

Proceeding on to Sharpitor Tor, a little to the R. is the beautiful cone of Leather Tor, which is very easily ascended from its N. side. The E. and S. sides are covered with some of the most remarkable clitters of rocks on the moor. Descend either by the footpath on the S.W. which leads to Vineylake, or on the N. side and follow the wall, which runs along below the tor, to the road which leads to Leather Tor Farm. Nosworthy Bridge, which spans the Meavy, will be seen in the valley below.

X. 6. Dousland to Black Tor Antiquities.

Continue walk (X. 4) to the bottom of the hill, and at the bend of the road beyond is a green road which leads to Stanlake. Keep on the Princetown road beyond this road to the bottom of the next hill.   Then take to the moor, and strike the wall to the E.   On the E. side of this wall runs a **very fine stone row,** which has been robbed to build the wall, but there is still a very good row left, and it

VIXEN TOR.

ends in a very substantial blocking-stone at its N. end; apparently it was a double row, and one of the rows is buried in the wall for support.

Mr. Baring-Gould told me that a very fine kistvaen once stood near here on the W. of Black Tor, but it was destroyed by the road menders.

Harter Tor stone rows can be seen from the tor on the opposite side of the Meavy, running down to the river.

They consist of two fine rows.   One is mutilated, but

they terminate in circles which formerly enclosed cairns.

An old tinner's blowing house is down below by the river side.

X. 7. **Leat Falls.** Continuing one's walk from where walk (6) terminated, a torrent rushes down from the moor in a succession of cascades just below the stone rows, and joins the Meavy. It is a beautiful spot.

Lower down are the Leat falls, where the Devonport leat comes tumbling and foaming down the hillside in a fine cascade, before it crosses the river through the acqueduct.

X. 8. **Nosworthy Bridge** is reached by Lowery.

40, 21, 21A, 8A.

The walk may be continued to Deancombe and Down Tor.

X. 9. **Round Leather Tor.** After passing Lowery cottage the road forks to the right. It leads to Nosworthy Bridge. To the left to Leather Tor Farm. Follow the road to the left till the leat crosses the road. Then follow the leat up for some distance and leave it where it enters a field ; here take the wall as your guide and rejoin the Princetown road, but keep on the high ground and visit the very fine hut circles on N.E. slopes of Sharpitor.

The brawling leat above Leather Tor Farm, with the tor in the background, presents a fine piece of mountain scenery.   40, 21, 21A.   40.

X. 10. **Crazywell Pool.** *Via* Lowery and Leather Tor Bridge.

40, 21, 21A, 21B, 21C.   8B, 8, 7, 2, 1.

X. 11. **Brisworthy Circle.** *Via* Marchant's Cross and Lynch Hill.

1, 39A, 11, 21, 22.

I cannot conclude these brief notes of Sheepstor without putting in a plea for the preservation of the ferns. Let the visitor if he will carry away bunches of the pink heath and heather, even the luck bearing white heather, if he can find it ; handfuls of golden water marigold *—drunkards* the people call them, though they drink water only—wild roses, if they do not mind scratching their fingers; the pretty little marsh violet, the round-leafed sundew, the broom, the golden saxifrage, the pretty luck-bean and the field gentian, but let them spare the ferns that they tear up by the roots. *Osmunda regalis* once grew by the streams, throwing its fronds six feet high—now |it is utterly eradicated. The two *Hymenophylla*, once so abundant in the Plym upper valley and in the roads near Meavy, can now scarcely be met with; the little oak fern is extremely rare. They are torn up and carried away— to die.

CONVICT PRISON, PRINCETOWN.

CHAPTER XI.

PRINCETOWN.

1—*Ingra Tor.* 2—*Merrivale.* 3—*Vixen Tor.* 4—*Staple and Cox Tors.* 5—*Great and Fur Tors.* 6—*Nun's Cross.* 7—*Fox Tor and Child's Tomb.* 8—*Crazywell Pool.* 9—*Nillacombe Valley.* 10—*Leather Tor.*

Princetown is the highest town in England and stands 1,400 ft. above sea level, near the base of North Hessary Tor. The air is very bracing and invigorating. It is a very good centre for exploring the moor, especially for

motorists, as the roads are excellent.   They will find
most comfortable head-quarters at the Duchy Hotel,
which is very up-to-date and exceedingly well managed.
The King and Queen stayed here a few days, when, as
Prince and Princess of Wales they visited their tenants in
the Duchy in June, 1910.

The Prison.   The great convict prison which our fellow-
countrymen all over the land associate with Dartmoor,
was built very early in the nineteenth century.   The
foundation stone was laid on March 20th, 1806, and the
buildings were very quickly erected.   It was built for a
military prison, and it was soon crowded to overflowing
with prisoners of war, of whom the greater number were
Frenchmen, captured during the great war with Napoleon
which closed with his defeat at Waterloo.   The prisoners
loudly complained about the severity of the Dartmoor
winter; and no wonder, for many of them had the misfortune to be securely lodged in Dartmoor prison during
the greatest frost England has experienced in modern
times—which continued with great persistency during the
first three months of 1814.   Escapes are now rare.

An assize has recently been concluded at Princetown
and 23 convicts sentenced for various periods for mutiny.

XI. 1.   **To Peak Hill and Ingra Tor.**   Take the Plymouth
road.   2 m. from Princetown a very fine piece of mountain
scenery lies before you.   The tors on L. of the road are
Sheep's Tor, Leather Tor and Sharpitor.   Ascending Peak
Hill, L. is a road to Stanlake Farm in Meavy Valley.   R.
are some roadmen's stone quarries and heaps.   Here turn
R. and cross the moor for Leeden Tor.   Either cross the
tor or make your way along its western slopes for Ingra
Tor.   About 300 yds. E. of Ingra Tor is a fine kistvaen
which has not been disturbed, except that a portion of the
capstone has been broken off.   This old monument is
known to very few people.   It was originally covered by
a mound, as so many are, a portion of which still remains.

From Ingra Tor the Walkham Valley is most picturesque.   In the autumn the foliage of the Walkham Woods
is gorgeous.

Cross the railway E. of Ingra Tor; then cross the little valley and pass over the railway crossing at the foot of King Tor. The Halt is here. Beyond the railway is a path which leads back to Princetown

XI. 2. **Merrivale Bridge** (3 m.) Either by the Tavistock road, or strike across the moor from the station, across the shoulder of N. Hessary Tor. It is a rough walk across the moor, as there is no track, but it is well worth the extra effort. A little stream with huge boulders in its course is struck $1\frac{1}{2}$ m. from the tor. Thence ascend the rising ground and the antiquities are in front of you.

MERRIVALE BRIDGE.

Merrivale Avenues consist of two long stone rows. They run E. and W. parallel to each other, 105 ft. apart, the longest 1,143 ft. and the other nearly 800 ft. The former has the remains of a circle in the centre.

Merrivale Kistvaen is a very large one. The capstone was mutilated by a farmer in 1860, who cut a gate post out of the middle of it.

Merrivale Longstone is seen S.W. of the Avenues and is 12 ft. high. It is a conspicuous object in the distance A smaller menhir is near by.

Merrivale Circle, a small circle with 8 stones, close to the Longstone. It formerly enclosed a kistvaen. Its diameter is 67 ft. These remains and others close by suffered severely when the new-take wall was built.

The Apple-crusher will be found among the hut circles. It is a circular stone cut out ready for use in the cider press, but it was never removed.

The Prehistoric Village lies between the road and the avenues. Many of the hut dwellings are large and well preserved. This group of hut circles is known locally as the *Plague Market.* Here, when Tavistock was being ravaged by the plague in 1625, in which year its mortality rose to 575, the farmers brought provisions and placed them for the people of Tavistock to take away, who left money in payment for the produce received at an appointed place. The same thing was done at Eyam in Derbyshire in 1665.

The huts were built by courses of stones placed one above another. The roof was formed by poles thatched over At the point where the poles converged, a cap was fitted in made of a hollowed stone. Specimens of these stones have occasionally been found. The doorway was formed by two jambs with a lintel. The latter are frequently still in position.

As one descends the road towards the bridge, below the 5 milestone the road makes a bend. Here a foot-track cuts across the moor and rejoins the road below. This passes through the groups of hut circles. From the antiquities descend to the bridge.

Merrivale Bridge is comparatively new. The old clapper bridge was swept away in a great flood during a thunderstorm in July, 1890. This storm caused freshets in several

of the Dartmoor streams and carried away many bridges.
There was a memorable flood at Peter Tavy on that
occasion.   A stroll up the Walkham is very pleasant;
there are three Blowing Houses on the E. side of the
stream.   It is a fine trout stream.   The fishing rights
belong to the Dartmoor Angling Association.

XI. 3   **Vixen Tor** is the fine pile of rocks on the L.
above the Walkham Valley.   It will be unwise to attempt
to reach it by a short cut from the bridge, as the ground
is very swampy.

LANGSTONE CIRCLE.

Ascend the hill past the quarries.   When the top of the
hill has been gained, a footpath branches off to the L.
towards the tor and runs parallel with a new-take wall.

The tor is the private property of Mr. Parsons, who
lives in the house at the foot of the tor.   It has been
owned by his family for 200 years.   He kindly allows
visitors to visit the tor.   Of late years so much trouble
has been given by thoughtless people, who strew the
ground around the tor with paper and broken bottles, that
closing the tor to visitors and picnic parties has been
under consideration.

The writer pleads with all sorts and conditions of
visitors not to leave bottles and refuse about the tor, but

to respect the owner's rights, so that no restrictions on the present privileges the public enjoy may be necessary. Do as you would be done by.

Vixen Tor Kistvaen will be found on the N. of the tor near the wall; it is 4 ft. by 1 ft. 9 in. One side stone is 5 ft. in length.

XI. 4. **Great Staple Tor.** There is a lane just above the inn which turns up to Shillapark Farm. Follow this a short distance, then strike across the moor for the tor, or keep to the Tavistock road to the top of the hill, and then branch off across the moor to the tors.

SWINCOMBE FARM.

The first tor approached is **Little Staple Tor.** Next comes **Middle Staple Tor,** and about ½ m. further on is **Great Staple Tor.** On Great Staple Tor the rocks have weathered into strange shapes. There is a tolmen on this tor.

The eminence westward across the boggy valley is **Cox Tor,** on which are several cairns. Nearly 400 yds. N. of the summit is a very large one. 200 yds. N.N.W. of this one are two very curious ring cairns; one has a diameter of 55 ft. and the other 27 ft. On the S. slope of the tor, 200 ft. below the summit, there is a cluster of small cairns.

Roos Tor formerly was crowned by a fine logan rock, which was mischievously destroyed by quarrymen a generation ago.

From Roos Tor are two very pleasant routes for returning. *Either* steer N.W. and strike the delightful coombe of Peter Tavy, down which the Peter Tavy Brook rushes and babbles over its rocky bed as it hurries on its way to meet the Tavy.

About 1 m. from Roos Tor are clusters of prehistoric huts, which have formed quite a little town ; *or* from the tor steer N.E. on to Langstone Moor, where **The Langstone** keeps its solitary watch over the plain. It is 12 ft. high. The Langstone was formerly the end of a stone row, composed of quite small stones, running in a direction N. and S. from a pool that occupies the site of a destroyed cairn. Nearly parallel to it, and 60 yds. away, was another row. The stone is composed of local gabbro, and was formerly prostrate, but His Grace the Duke of Bedford has re-erected it in its original socket-hole. The old lych way ran from Whittenburrow to it, and then passed on to Cudlip Town.

Looking E. from the Langstone, about $\frac{1}{2}$ m. distant will be seen the **Langstone Circle,** which is a fine specimen of this class of monument, which I have explained in my book on the Land's End (No. 5, pp. 89-91). It was discovered as recently as 1894. Not a single stone was then standing, but fortunately none had been taken away or even mutilated. The Duke of Bedford kindly allowed the stones to be re-erected, and supplied the men to do the work, which was directed by the late Rev. S. Baring-Gould and the late Mr. Robert Burnard. It has 16 stones, and its diameter is about 60 ft. There was originally another circle outside this one, of which only two or three stones remain.

From the circle one can cross the Walkham by Greena-ball to Mis Tor, and from there return to Princetown.

XI. 5. **Great Mis Tor** is a very easy excursion from Princetown. Take the Tavistock road to Rundlestone, then turn up the rough road to the R. by the cottages.

Here a wall is your companion for some distance ; when it parts company with you, strike for the tor. **Fice's Well,** which bears the date 1568, is now within the prison lands. On the E. side of the prison leat is the new-take wall of the prison farm, running N. and S. The well is over the wall, close to that portion of the wall which runs in an E. direction.

Photo by]   *[R. Hansford Worth.*
RE-ERECTING BRISWORTHY CIRCLE.—*See page* 23.

Beardown Clapper Bridge, Beardown Man on Devil Tor, and Wistman's Wood I have described in my chapter on Two Bridges (No. 2, IX. 3-9). At Mis Tor is Mis Tor Pan.

It is only a short distance from Great Mis Tor to **Fur Tor** (1,877 ft.), an island of firm ground rising in the midst of a sea of almost impassable bogs, through which Fur Tor Cut passes, which is the way across the bogs used by moormen for removing their cattle.

XI. 6. Nun's Cross Farm. *Either* take the road past Tor Royal, and at the point where it turns L. to Whiteworks, take the rough track which runs nearly due S.; *or* take the path behind the " Plume of Feathers " which leads to South Hessary Tor, whence keep on the ridge which trends S.S.E. Nun's Cross will be found where this ridge ends. It is situated on a neck of land which separates the Nillacombe and Swincombe Valleys.

On the W. side of the new-take wall is Nun's Cross, which was one of a long line of crosses which marked the monks' trackway connecting Buckfastleigh with Buckfast Abbey. It bears the inscriptions: *Crux Siwardi*; *Bocland*. The cross was thrown down and broken 90 years ago, but the late Sir Ralph Lopes, in 1846, took compassion on the fractured and prostrate form of this symbol of the Faith and had it mended and re-erected.

One can proceed on to Eylesbarrow. From the cairns on the highest point is one of the finest views in the Southern Quarter. On reaching the ruined building of the old mine, turn to the R., follow the track, and return by Sheepstor to Dousland Station.

The distance from Princetown to Nun's Cross, Eylesbarrow, Sheepstor and Dousland is 11 m.

XI. 7. Fox Tor and Child's Tomb (1 m. E. of Nun's Cross). Fox Tor is not a conspicuous tor. It crowns a rugged elongated hill which stretches down to Fox Tor Mire, a very formidable swamp, where one of the few escapes from Princetown disappeared and was never heard of again. There is a safe path across the mire from Fox Tor to Whiteworks. The low bank which is seen winding

across the flat ground from the white gate below the tor
marks it.

When I was approaching Child's Tomb one day in
May, 1912, the largest fox that I have ever seen on Dartmoor sprang up out of the heather, and after leaping
across the wall, it ran leisurely over the top of Fox Tor.

Fox Tor Brook is a delightful torrent which takes its
rise in Cater's Beam and flows among the rocks on the
highest ground of Fox Tor, and descends into the Swin-

FOX TOR MIRE.

combe Valley in a succession of small but charming
cascades.

A Ruined Kistvaen. About 1 m. E. of Nun's Cross Farm,
on the W. side of the dip formed by a lateral stream of
the Swincombe, are the remains of this kistvaen. A block
of white spa will be seen in the wall which is one's companion from Nun's Cross to Fox Tor. The kistvaen lies
about 60 yds. S.E. of the white spa, and about 45 yds. in
a direct line from the wall.

Child's Tomb. Looking down from Fox Tor are two
little depressions, through which flow streamlets—feeders
of the Swincombe—which unite before reaching the latter.

On the little ridge which separates these streams, about

half-way between them, and a $\frac{1}{4}$ m. due N. of the Tor, is
Child's Tomb. It is the ruin of a kistvaen. Connected
with it is the well-known legend of Child the Hunter, who
must have lived at Plymstock before the Norman Con-
quest, because in the Domesday Book the lands in
Plymstock are recorded as belonging to the Abbey of
Tavistock. The story probably refers to a much earlier
legend, and is an instance of those strange legends which
are sometimes met with. The Welsh legend of Llewellyn's
hound is another instance, which finds its counterpart in
other lands.

The story of Child is that his horse became stogged in
Fox Tor Mire, and he was overtaken by a snowstorm and
perished on the moor. Before he died, he killed his horse
and crept inside the animal for warmth, and wrote his
will in the animal's blood :

> "The first that finds and brings me to my grave,
> My lands in Plymstock they shall have"

The monks of Tavistock, greedy of gain, hearing of the
last will and testament of Child, started at once for the
moor and found his lifeless body. On returning to the
town, they heard that the monks of Plymstock were
waiting at a ford to intercept them. The wily monks
changed their course and threw a bridge across the river
near the abbey, known to this day as Guile Bridge, and
reached the abbey in safety, and gained possession of the
lands in Plymstock.

XI. 8. **Crazywell Pool** is 3 m. S. of Princetown (No. 1.
V. 4). The most direct way is to go to Cramber Tor.
There is a delightful walk from Cramber Tor to Down
Tor, Deancombe and the Drizzlecombe Antiquities—

> " O'er the rills and the crags and the hills."

The course from Cramber should be set due S. The
beautiful valleys of the Nillacombe and Dean are crossed.
The pedestrian should return through Sheepstor to Dousland Station. From Cramber Tor the Pool is a short mile
distant S.S.W. Keep well up because of the swampy
valley. The Devonport leat runs above the Pool, and
should be crossed by a footbridge which will be found
quite near the Pool.

Another route, if one wants a longer walk, is to follow the rough road to Whiteworks, and then to take the rough cart track which branches off to R. and runs just above Kingset.   On this mountain track one may often see—

> " A flock of sheep that leisurely pass by,
>   One after another."

In the valley below flows the Nillacombe, or Newley-combe.   Through the combe beyond Down Tor is the Dean, which is mentioned in a charter of Isabella de Fortibus, dated 1291 :

> " Still glides the stream, and shall for ever glide ;
>   The form remains, the function never dies "

FALLS ON THE MEAVY BELOW BLACK TOR.

XI. 9.   **The Nilla-combe Valley.**   From Nosworthy Bridge *either* take the green lane up to Kingset and from there descend into the valley, *or* follow up the Nilla-combe, which joins the Meavy below the bridge.   It is a rocky valley, but higher up the stream, beyond Kingset, are peeps of great beauty.   All the way up the ground has been turned over and over by the tin-streamers, whose heaps of refuse are seen everywhere.

The Nillacombe takes its rise in quite a small spring at the head of the valley, but—

> " Large streams from little fountains flow."

and a little trickle soon expands into a brawling stream.

XI. 10. **Leather Tor and Nosworthy Bridge** (4½ m.) Take the Plymouth road to the point where the road goes down to Stanlake Farm. Here branch off across the moor, keeping Leather Tor on your R. hand. There are some large and very perfect hut circles on the N. slopes of the tor. As one approaches the tor, the Devonport leat is struck. The leat becomes a fine mountain torrent as it flows below Leather Tor, and rushes over the boulders with great tumult. Leather Tor Bridge spans the Meavy below Leather Tor Farm, and the view from the W. side is very picturesque. Above the bridge, on the E. bank of the stream, are the remains of an old blowing house.

From Leather Tor Farm take the road which leads up the hill ; it soon crosses the leat. Keep to the road till it turns sharply to the L. Here is Lowery Cross with its massive base. This lane will soon lead you to Nosworthy Bridge. Below the bridge the Meavy is joined by the Nillacombe, and it is rather a noisy meeting, especially after heavy rain. Further up the road towards Narrator the Dean comes down the valley and flows into the Meavy.

It is a land of streams just here. Very pleasant it is to listen to —
           " The brooks;
      Muttering along the stones, a busy noise
      By day, a quiet sound in silent night."

The view from Nosworthy Bridge, looking up stream, is one of extreme beauty. With the brawling river in the foreground and the cone of Leather Tor soaring up in the background, it assumes the proportions of real grandeur, and is, I believe, the finest piece of real mountain scenery on the moor.

Among the trees on the R. are the ruins of Nosworthy Farm. On the E. bank of the river, about 100 yds. above the farm, where the path becomes narrow, you will come upon traces of the walls of an old shed. Here are nearly a dozen round hollows cut in the rocks, which were the old slag pounding hollows used by the tinners.

CHAPTER XII.

YELVERTON.

1—Meavy. 2—Bickleigh Vale. 3—Roborough Down.

Yelverton is built around a breezy common, and is in a most healthy situation. With such a fine expanse of common, Yelverton folk can never complain of over-crowding or of any lack of fresh air. Of late years, Yelverton has attracted an increasing number of visitors, who come to enjoy the beautiful moors, for which it is a good centre.

It stands on high ground, and has a much more genial climate during the winter months than is experienced further on Dartmoor. In winter at Sheepstor the snow sometimes covers the ground for days, when there is very little to be seen at Dousland or Yelverton. The place is also blessed with a good deal of sunshine ; it has an appreciably higher record than places further inland.

With the exception of the walks which I mention below, all the beautiful walks accessible from Yelverton are fully described in Chapters IX. and X. dealing with Sheepstor and Dousland, so walk or train to Dousland and start from there.

The other pleasant walks from Yelverton are as follows : —

XII. 1. **Meavy** (1½ m) Turn down the lane which runs parallel to the station road. When you approach the railway arch, turn, sharply under the railway. This lane will bring you straight into Meavy, which I described in my Dousland chapter.

XII. 2. **Bickleigh Vale.** Visitors to this neighbourhood should walk through Bickleigh Vale, through which the Plym flows. Here are sylvan peeps of real beauty. Alight at Plym Bridge Platform or Marsh Mills Station and walk up the Vale to Bickleigh Station.

There is also a pleasant walk beside the Meavy from Good-a-Meavy to Yelverton.

A visit may profitably be paid to Meavy. The church is in a very good condition of repair, and contains some very early carving at the chancel arch, that may be pre-Norman, so rude is it.   Near the church is an old house of the Drake family, now a farm, and the village cross, and the famous Meavy oak, 27 ft. in circumference, with the trunk so decayed as to form an archway through which a person may walk erect.   It is supposed to have been standing here in the reign of King John.   The village chronicles relate that nine persons once dined within the hollow trunk, where a peat-stack may now be frequently seen, piled up as winter fuel.   Although the head of the tree be bald, the lower branches are still bright with foliage.

In the churchyard is an epitaph, a varient of others found elsewhere :—

> Our life is but a winter's day ;
> Some only breakfast, and then away :
> Others to dinner stay, and are full fed,
> The oldest man but sups and goes to bed.
> Large is his debt who lingers out the day ;
> Who goes the soonest has the least to pay.

The point here is that the stone commemorates the members of a family who died at the respective ages of 94, 88, 29 and 16.

XII, 3. **Roborough Down** is a fine tract of moor for a ramble. Roborough Rocks are passed on the right – a favourite picnic place for visitors. There are excellent golf links on Roborough Down at the Yelverton end.

CHAPTER XIII.

Some Dartmoor Worthies.

SIR JAMES BROOKE, First Rajah of Sarawak   A good account of his life appears in " Beautiful Dartmoor," Part I. which I will not repeat here; but I had some good notes

RAJAH BROOKE PARLEYING WITH THE NATIVE RAJAH
WHO PRECEDED HIM.

about him given me by Mr. Charles Calmady, of Horra-bridge, who, when he was a boy, knew him well. He says:—"He was a man of a very distinguished appearance, about 5 ft. 10 ins. in height, with a slight but well proportioned figure. His complexion was sallow, and his face rather heavily pitted with small pox. One day we went to call at Burrator House, and he introduced us to Mr. and Mrs. Cruickshank who were staying with him. He placed his hand on my shoulder and pointing to Mrs. Cruickshank, said—' that lady standing there has the mark of a cut from a Chinese sword all down her back.' "

The circumstances were:—
One day the Sarawak Residency was suddenly surrounded by a band of Chinese Rebels, and being taken completely by surprise, the Rajah and his friends had to fly for their lives. Both the Cruickshanks were cut down and left for dead. The Rajah and a few followers succeeded in escaping by wading through what was thought to be an impassible swamp, and in an incredibly short time he gathered an armed force, and before the rebels had time to make off with the loot, he surrounded the Residency and slaughtered every Chinaman he could find. He was in time to save the Cruickshanks, who, though left for dead were still alive.
Under medical care they both recovered and returned to England.

Mr. Calmady says he thinks he must be the only person alive to have attended the Rajah's funeral in 1868, but

Mr. Amos Shillibeer still living in Sheepstor was there.

The Rajah's Tomb is in the N.E. corner of Sheepstor Churchyard under the shade of the great beech tree, and is made of red Aberdeen Granite.

He was a very remarkable man, and made Sarawak what it is, and his work has been so splendidly carried on by the second and third Rajah's.

RAJAH BROOKE

FIRST RAJAH BROOK'S TOMB AT SHEEPSTOR.

THE SECOND RAJAH was buried by myself in August, 1921, two years after he died. The War Laws were still in force, tho' the war was actually over when he died, and the Government of the day would not allow his enbalmed body to be taken to Sarawak. The idea was to have an impressive funeral there to impress the Natives, but after two years it was felt certain the natives with their primitive minds would have forgotten he ever lived. So at last it was decided to bury him at Sheepstor. The present Rajah and Rajnee, and the widow were present at the funeral. The coffin which was made of very fine grained Sarawak wood, arrived the previous evening, and remained in the Church till the time of the funeral next day.

The grey granite forming the tomb was quarried in Sheep's Tor, and drawn down to the Churchyard by eleven horses, and through the Churchyard wall. It was cracked on the way down, so great a mass of granite is often liable to crack in this way.

HARRY TERRELL.

HARRY TERRELL was a remarkable man in many ways. He was a simple child of nature and an accomplished horseman, a great hunter of fox and fulmart. He lived for many years at Burrator House, and finally sold it to the 1st Rajah Brooke. I could tell many tales of him, but lack of space prevents me giving more than one, in which he succeeded in deceiving that wily huntsman—the Rev. John Russell—Russell brought his hounds from North Devon for a week's hunting in the south. Foxes were scarce in those days, and there was some fear that there might be a blank day. Jack Russell was on such intimate terms with his hounds that the least variation in the behaviour of any one of them would attract his attention.

There is a peculiarity in the scent of a bagged fox; if he has only been captured a short time he is not like a wild fox, and a great change has come over him which affects the scent he leaves behind him.

A confidential man with a bagged fox was instructed to lie down in the middle of a very thick brake. When he heard Russell's horn, on leaving the meet, about $\frac{1}{4}$ mile off, he was to let go the fox and then lie quite still and quiet himself, until everyone was gone.

The hounds were thrown into one end of the brake and gradually drawn up to the fox, and a Billy Black was outside to view him away and distract attention by a superabundant amount of hallooing. The hounds settled on their line and travelled right across Dartmoor and killed in the open. They eat their fox, and Russell never knew he had been cheated with a bagged fox, but always talked of it as a perfect run. He was never told.

Terrell was born in Tavistock, on 12th April, in 1807, and died in London, March 18th, 1871.

JOHNNY ROBERTS was a mighty huntsman and an especially fine rider, and was huntsman of Mr. Pode's hounds, of Slade, Cornwood.

There is an absurd story of a great run, when Johnny Roberts rode his horse to a stand still, no one else up; he took a promising looking horse out of a plough – no ploughman would think of refusing Johnny anything, and finished the run on him bareback, the only one at the death. Johnny left behind him an immense reputation.

Some of the old hunting-men were perpetually referring to " Johnny Roberts' Day " with lamentations for a time of perfect, happy hunting, past and gone, never to be seen again.

A very large fox had been driven to earth and it was decided to take him out, which was a formidable undertaking. Terrell's white rough terrier was " in " and

they had to dig to her. As she never ceased fighting the
fox, and "telling" about him, they could only dig to her
"noising."

A dispute arose, and Terrell gave a very decided
opinion, on which a well-known hunting man said :—

"Ah ! it would not have been like that in Johnny Roberts'
day. Terrell said, 'I was sartain Johnny Roberts would
be drawed in my teeth. Johnny Roberts was a good
sportsman, I've no doubt, but he had a forgitful lot of
disciples.'"

They dug on and took out the fox, which had a huge
mask and was very old.

RICHARD LAVERS OF TROWLESWORTHY.

RICHARD LAVERS. This fine old man lived at
Trowlesworthy Warren for a great number of years. I
knew him only in the later years of his life.

He was a wonderfully sturdy man, and a fine type of
moorman. He took a keen interest in Freemasonry, and

was possibly the oldest Mason in Devon. He was a member of Lodge " Erme " 1091, Ivybridge, and for a very long period attended the Meetings. He died on March 15th, 1915, and was buried on March 20th.

The morning brought a very deep drifting snow but the March sun melted 3 ft. in a day. His coffin which was in a hearse was preceded by a long line of outriders on horseback, and the procession was a most dignified affair.

On that day Richard no doubt had his wish fulfilled. About two years before he died he paid a visit to the Vicar of Shaugh, and said he had one request he wanted the Vicar to grant.

" When I die, will you be sure and bury me beside my first wife." The reply was—" Of course I will."

CHAPTER XIV.

Ancient Records of Dartmoor Parishes

PART 2.

CHURCHWARDENS' ACCOUNTS, 1567—1600.

These are contained in a book in a bad condition, and disreputable appearance.

The earliest book, which dates 1567 to 1602, has four separate Accounts each year and few are missing—First comes the Churchwardens' Accounts; then the Constables'—a very fine collection; then those of the Collectors for the Poor, and lastly the Surveyor's of the Wayes, the last named are in each case brief, but they contain an interesting account of the repairs of the highways and byways.

In dealing with a field so vast as the Parochial Records of nearly 400 years it is obviously only possible to give a few matters of interest.

The next book contains the Collectors' Accounts from 1611 to 1657. Then comes a serious gap to 1681, when the Churchwardens' and Constables' Accounts are renewed, but both are in the *same* account each year, from 1681 the Churchwardens' Accounts are continuous to the present day, and the Constables' Accounts 1681 to 1800.

Both are missing in the Civil Wars period. There are complete lists of Officers—The iiij men from 1565 to 1600: the Churchwarden's 1554 to 1628 (and on to the present day in the Accounts); also a complete list of the Collectors of the Poor, 1568 to 1629; also of the Surveyors of the Wayes, 1569 to 1628.

The Altar.

Early in the reign of Elizabeth an order was made for the removal of the stone altars and Dean Prior obeyed the order, the stone was to be replaced by a table of wood.

1568. For wryting the X Commandments —xxvs.
Pd for makyn of the Communyon Tabell.—xd.
Pd for iiij crooks of iron for the same tabell.—

E

The altar stone was sold in the following year.

1569.   Received for our Alter stone.—iijs. iiijd.
1576.   Payed for the Communyon Cuppe.—xxijs. ijd.

This date agrees with the date inscribed on the cover of our Chalice, which was made at this time by Johns, a famous silversmith at Exeter in Elizabethan times.

At some time the bowl has been broken from the stem of the Cup.

1591.   Pd for mendying of the Communyon Cuppe. ijd.
1573.   Pd for ij coverynges for the Communyon Tabell —iijs. iiijd.
1583.   Pd for wayssynge of the Church Ornements for iij several tymes.—iijd.
1585.   Pd for a glassen bottell.—iijd.
1586.   Wasshyn of the communyon clothe.
1595.   Pd for a forme in the Chancel. – xd.
1571.   Pd for a but (hassock) to lye before the Communyon tabell.—ijd.

The amount of wine used at Dean was always moderate.

1575.   Pd for wine for the Communyon.—ijd.
1581.   Pd for a bottell to keep wyne in.—6d.
1581.   Pd for a boxse to keep bryde in.—6d.
1581   Pd for the Syngen bred.– js.

This was the larger or priest's wafer ; it is said to have been called the singing Bread because chants were sung while it was being made. This shows that the wafer was not forbidden at the Reformation, but it was still in use in 1581 ; support of this is seen in the smallness of the cover of our 1576 chalice. This small paten was made expressly for the use of the wafer.

At Tavistock 36 quarts were used at Easter. The quantity used in many parishes was a constant source of strife between the parish priest and the churchwardens. The quantity required at the Celebration of the Communion was used, and the bulk went into the priest's cellar ; this is a liquid fact.

Recently, I was going through the Warden's Account of a Devon parish, date 1800. There was strife between the priest and churchwardens, and the priest claimed his wine on the ground of " Immemorial custom " and won his point. Henceforth, for many years, there was this charge—" *Pd to the minister in room of wine according to custom—£1 4s. od.*" A monstrous imposition.

The Font.

Dean Font is Norman, made of Devon red sandstone. It was painted once, why I cannot think, unless it was before the present lead lining was placed in it, and that the stone was porous.

1682. Pd for painting the King's Arms and setting up the sittenes in the Church and painting the pulpit and desk and vant.— £8 18s. 0d.

It was customary in preparing for Baptism, after the Cover had been unlocked and raised, to cover the font with a fair linen cloth. References to " *the font cloth* " are very rare in Wardens' Accounts. Dean has two such references.

1586. Wasshynge the vant cloth.—jd.
1597. Washynge the vant clothe.—jd.

During the Commonwealth the use of the font was forbidden and a pewter basin substituted. Dean still has its pewter basin.

Gifts.

Sometimes the Church Account was helped by gifts of money.

The Church made many gifts to Church building, &c.

1576. For the charge of the buldynge of the castell of Exon.—ijs.
1577. The Collections for the buldynge of the Church of Bath.—xijd.
1569. Pd to the relefe of them taken in Turkey.—xxd.
1577. Pd to iij other collectors of severall hospetalles.—xiijd.
1586. Pd towards the re-edifying of a Church in London.- xjd.

VISITATIONS DURING THIS PERIOD.

The Archdeacon's Visitation is Annual, and the Bishop's very frequent.

1567. Expenses at the Bishop's Vysytasion.
1567. Charge and Expense at the Archdecon's Vysytasion.—iijs.
1568. Pd for expenses at the Archdecon's Vysytasion.—ijs. ixd.
1574. Pd at the Bishop's Vysytacion.—iijs. ijd.
*1576. Pd at the bysshope (Archbishop) of Canterbury's Vysitation — vjs. iiijd.
    Pd to the bysshope of Canterbury's Officers.—xijd.
1577. Pd at the bysshoppes vysytacion.—iiijs.
    Pd more at Exon at the bysshoppe's curte (court)—iijs. iijd.
1583. Pd at the Archdeacon's Vysitatyon at Totnes and for our Articles and all other charges.—vs.
*1584. Pd at the Bysshop's Vysytacion of Canterye hodenn at Totynyes and for our expenses.—iiijs.
    Pd at the Archdekens Vysytacion.

1595.   Pd for our Artikelles at the Vysytacion.—js. iiijd.
        Pd for a collage in Kingston on Thems.—xd.
1599.   Pd for our Artikelles at the Visytayon.—js.

" *The Articles* " were " The Articles of Enquiry "
relating to the conduct of the Incumbent and the conduct
of the services during the past year, and other business.

* The Woodleigh Parish Books record these visitations
of the Archbishop, and a third in 1634 by Archbishop
Land.

The Office of Rural Dean was not instituted until 16—

The Bells.

In the Tudor Period, Dean Prior had four bells which
were old bells in 1567, when our Accounts begin; they
are recorded in the Certificate of the Parish goods issued
to the Church in 1553. (*See Part 2, Page 1.*)

These four bells were re-cast in 1734, evidently at the
expense of the Yarde family.

Here are some interesting stories :—

1568.   Casting of the lytel bell, xijs. viijd.   For setting up of the
        bell.—ijs. vjd.
        Pd to Robert Tolchard for mendyng and kepyng of the Bells.
        xiijd.
1569.   Pd for makynge the jar (iron) work of the littell bell.—vjd.
1593.   Pd John Tolchard for mendynge of the bell-frame and for
        grese,—xd.
        Pd for a bell coller and for a pott of oyle.—vjd.
1595.   Pd to the Ringers on the Crownatyon (Coronation) Daye.
        —iijs. vjd.
        Pd for grese and oyle for the bells.—iiijd.
        Pd to Robert Tolchard for Kepynge of the Bells.—ijs. vjd.
1597.   Pd to the Ringers the 17th day November.—xxd.
                (Queen's Birthday.)

Books.

1568.   Pd for a Communyon Booke.—viijd.
1570.   Pd for an homelye booke.—xvjd.
1576.   Pd for a newe homelye book.—xvjd.
1582.   Pd for six littell books.—vjd.
1589.   Pd for mendynge of the Church books, viz. : the bebell and
        the too communyon bookes.—iijs. iiijd.
1592.   Pd for a new bending (binding) of the Communyon booke.—
        ijs. vjd.
1597.   Pd for a bourck of prayers for her Majestye fflett.—iijs.

Robes.

1573. Pd for a Serpeles and a Rouchett (Rochet).—xviijs.

Church Repairs and Renewals.

1567. Pd for 2,000 lathe nayles.—iijs.
,, 1,500 shyndle pynnes.—iijs.
,. 1,000 shyndle stones (slates).—ijs.
1568. Pd for brode stones for the Church.—ijs. vjd.
,, fetching home the same.—vijd.
,, mendynge the Church geate.—ixd.
1569. Pd more for the iron work of the Church Geate.—vjd.
Pd for lying and mendynge of the leddes.—xxxiijs. xd.
1574. Pd for tylinge in the Church.—ijd. (Two tiles only remain).
1576. Pd the glassyer for mendynge and glassynge our Church wyndows.—xxxs.
1584. Pd for mendynge of the stepel dore locke and the Church dore locke.
1588. Pd to the glassyer for putten newe glass and mendynge of our Church wyndons.—xvjs. viijd.
1590. Pd for a new cheste his locke, and kaye, and hemes (iron bands)—xiijs. vijd.
1592. Pd for glassynge of the Church windowes.—vjs. iiijd.
1593. Pd for a ladder for the puyche.
,, mendynge the sigge (seat) behend the Church dore.
(This was there till the last restoration).
Pd more for tomber for the same.—iiijs.
1594. Pd Would the plumbmer.—iljd.
Pd to the plomber and carpenter for coming at severall tymes and expenses —ijs. xd.
Pd for bryngynge some of the new ledde and for carydge back of the old ledde and expense.—xijs. vjd.
Pd for expense when we weyhed the old ledde.—iiijd.
Pd the carpenter for worke for the leddes.—xs. vjd.
Pd for tymber and expenses.—xiijs.

(1). SOURCES OF THE INCOME FOR CHURCH EXPENSES.

THE CHURCH ALE was not, as is often assumed, a parish drunk, but a perfectly legitimate day's enjoyment. It was the parish feast, and drinking old English Ale played a part in it; some disgraced themselves as they do now, by taking too much.

These were the different ales held :—

The Ale was a periodical gathering of parishioners, which continued to be held into the eighteenth century. Its object was to raise funds through the medium of amusement. There were several kinds. I give the principal ones.

(1) **The Church Ale,** or Whitsun Ale, so called because from being generally held at Whitsuntide, was
quite an important institution. The two churchwardens
were the ale-givers, who, after collecting subscriptions in
money and kind from the parishioners, gave a revel.
This Ale was held in the Church House, wherein the
churchwardens brewed and stored their ale and gave a
feast, the proceeds of which were devoted to replenishing
church funds and repairing the church.

(2) **The Clerk Ale,** was a feast held to increase the
meagre salary of the parish clerk. It realized a fairly
substantial sum—more than his salary would amount to
in several years.

(3) **The Bid-Ale** was held when a parishioner had failed
in his worldly calling, or to use a Dartmoor expression,
gone scat ; or if he had met with an accident or some
other misfortune depriving him of his livelihood. The
Bid-Ale was not lacking in humour. With the proceeds
of the feast which were handed over to him, the broken
man was expected to make a feast of ale, and all that was
left after the expenses of the feast were paid went to the
unfortunate man to set him on his legs again for a renewed fight with the world.

(4) **Give-Ales,** were the legacies of individuals, and
entirely gratuitous.

(5) **Bride-Ale,** was sold by a bride on her wedding
day. She received whatever handsome price the guests
choose to pay her for it.

(6) **Foot-Ale.** was the feast, in which liquor flowed
freely, required from one entering on a new occupation.

(7) **Drink-lean,** was a contribution of tenants towards
a potation or ale provided to entertain the lord or his
steward.

There are still the remains of two Ale-Houses in this
neighbourhood—one at Rattery, near the churchyard
gate ; the other at Widecombe, which is now the Parish
Room.

Here I am dealing with The Church Ale, as a source of revenue for the Church Accounts and I give some instances at Dean.

1567.   Received of the Church Ale.—xl. viijs. 0d.
1569.   ,,   ,,   ,,   iiijl. iijs. iiijd.

They realised different amounts in different years as not only the Churchwardens, but also the iiij men organised an Ale, and sometimes they were held more than once a year.

1576.   The iiij men's Ale realised xl. viijs. ixd.
        The Wardens' Ale, iijl. viijs. 0d.

Compulsory Church Rates were unknown before Elizabeth's reign.

(2).   THE HIRE OF CHURCH PROPERTY.

Another regular source of income was the hire of the Church Vessell and other parish property for the purpose of private brewings. There are hundreds of these records.

1568.   Recd of Andrew Foxe for brewynge in the Church House.—
        xijd.
        Chrystopher Maddick for occupying the Chytell (the furnace)
        —vjd.
1580.   Recd from Chrystopher Arscot for hire of ye vessell.—vjd.
        (the iron pot in which the ale was brewed).

The rent of these articles produced quite a regular income for the Church as they were hired so much each year.

Another source of income was profits from the Church Farm.

1568.   Recd of Marjery Fell for a shepe.—iiijs. iiijd.

(3).   GIFTS.

Sometimes the Church Account was helped by gifts of money :—

1578.   Recd of the beneyvolence of the young men.—ijs. ijd.
1579.   Margery Mudge's gift to the poure.—iijs. iiijd.

(4).   SUNDRY SALES OF CHURCH PROPERTY.

1569.   Old tymber.—-iiijs. xd.
1573.   Olde Iron.—iii'd.
1581.   Recd for the Olde Bebell the sum of 3/-

(5).   THE CHURCH RATE.

See the Rating List for the Collectors of the Poor for 1589, given in the plates in "Robert Furze, Gentleman."

(6).   THE CHURCH PYTT.

For burial in the Church at a uniform charge of vjs. viijd.   (See Church Pytt, p. 97).

DEAN AND THE POPE.

Peter's Pence or Romescot dates back to the Saxon period, and a tax of a penny on every hearth was sent to Rome.   It was diverted to the Cathedrals by Henry VIII and ceased to be paid to Rome; restored by Mary, and again changed by Elizabeth.

It is called Peter's Farthings at Milton Abbot in 1588.

These were made at Dean long after they ceased in most parishes.

1582.   Pd for Peter's Pynce.—vid

It should be noted that vid. did not represent the amount paid to Peter.   A certain amount was fixed for the parish to pay, and the amount raised always fell short of the assessment and the deficit was made up from the Churchwarden's Accounts.   This vid. represents this deficit.

The monks of Buckfast recently made this amusing retort in "Chimes" : —

"We learn from *The Tablet* that our neighbour, the Anglican Vicar of Dean Prior, has just discovered in the churchwarden's accounts entries shewing the payment of Peter's Pence in that parish as late as 1597.   It is to be doubted whether the Pence, paid nearly 40 years after the accession of Elizabeth, ever found their way to Peter !   Possibly not."

There are frequent payments to Pardoners.   A Pardoner was one who went about with the Pope's Indulgences in his pocket to sell to the highest bidder.   The amounts of the payments differ at Dean.

1575.   Pd to a Pardner—occurs this year no less than four times.

Several generations later Dean evidently needed pardon.
1700.   Pd for a Proclamation against immorality and prophanesse.
   1s. 0d.

LIST OF THESE PAYMENTS.

1569. Pd for Peter's Rent.—vjd.
1570.   ,,   Pardon.—vjd.
1571.   ,,   ,,   vjd.
1575. Pd to a Pardener.—vjd. (4 men's Ale)
        ,,   Pardner   iiijd.
        ,,   Pardner   vjd.
        ,,   Pardner   vjd.
1580. Pd to a pure (poor) pardoner.—iiijd.
1582. Pd for Peter's Pynce.—vjd.
1584. At the Archedetions Vysytation at Tottnys Pd for our expenses and for Peter's Pardoner.—
1586. Pd for Peter's Pens.—vjd.
1592, Pd the Pardner. vjd.
1594. Pd to ix, Pardners at severall tyemes.—ijs, iiijd.
        Pd to ij pardners more —vjd.
1594. Pd for the lyenge in of our byll for the *recusant.*—xijd.
1595. Pd for Peter's Penes.—vjd.
1596. Pd for the lyeing in our bill and Peters Pens.—xd.
        Pd for a Pardoner that Voyse deleverd.—vjd.
1597.   ,,   Peters Penys and for lyeing in of our bill.—xd.
1594.   ,,   bringing in of our bill and Peters Pence.—js. od.

The Church Pytt.

This refers to the custom of burials under the Church floor.

This revolting and loathesome method of burial was much in use through Elizabeth's reign.

In consequence of these burials the Churches became regular pest houses, and were often the cause of the grave outbreaks of plague so common in those days.

For burials in the Church the charge over all England seems to have been the same,—vis. viijd.

Under the floor was called the Church Pytt.

There are many such records in Dean.

1568. Recd for Symon Mardale'c buriall in the Church Pytt.—vjs. viijd.
1574. Recd for Walter Tolchard's grave in the Pytt.—vjs. viijd.
1568. Johan Shere for her husband's buryal in the Church Pytt.—vjs. viijd
1569. S. Foxe   ditto
1581. Pd to John Dunridge for Christopher Voyse's ditto-vjs. viijd.
1578. Rd of Robert Furze for a grave for his sonne in the Church—vjs. viijd.
1581. Rd of Margerye Stidston for her father's grave in the Church.—vjs. viijd.

There is this curious record :

1597. Pd to . . . for makynge plene fo the walkes and the pet in the Church.—xd.

The Church floor was of earth ; this man levelled and made plain the paths, and also shewed where the burials were taking place then.

Outside the Church Porch on the west side, there is still an ossuary to which the bones were removed when the Church pytt became overcrowded. On Sundays Dean people sit in Church with their feet resting on the bones of their ancestors.

These Dean records show that there was uniformity to the Charges for ' buryall in ye Church Pytt,' the popular view was otherwise.

This is illustrated at Hartland, where there used to be this verse on a tomb some years ago :—

> " Here lies I at the Church Door ;
> Here lies I because I'se poor,
> The further in, the more they pay
> But here lies I as warm as they."

A distinction of this kind is hateful, but it is not confined to Christian times. A few years before I went to Alfriston, excavations for the foundations of a new house, revealed the site of an ancient Pagan burial ground, said to have been Saxon—the field was named " Sanctuary." The richer folk had been buried with their treasures in careful order, the poor had been thrown into a pit anyhow.

About 100 burials were located, and this feature was noticeable. Most of the finds are exhibited in the Lewes Museum now.

The Churchyard.

1568. Pd for mendynge of the Church Geate.—ixd.
1574. Pd for a rope for the Church Geate.—iijs
1572. Pd for makynge of the Church Yarthe Hagges.—ijs. ijd.
1586. Pd for makynge of the Church Yard hagge beside the wode.

(Before the road was widened there was a belt of trees at the west-end).

1586. Pd to Robt. Tolchard for mendynge the Churchyard geate. xijd.

Pd more for a springe for the Churchyard geate.—iiijd.

1580. Pd for mendynge of the polye (pulley) of the Church geate.

(This primitive form of opening and shutting a gate is still in use at Sheepstor. The rope often rots and has to be renewed, but the polye (pulley) lasts years.)

THE SORROWS OF DEAN.

At Dean in 1590, the plague carried off at least 50 people. There were 56 burials that year, 51 of which took place in the four months, July to October. This against the annual average of about 6 each year. One family was wiped out. There are these notes in the Register,--" Here the Plague began, ... here the Plague ended."

In 1678 there were 22 burials but there is no record of the nature of the outbreak.

In 1866 there was a grave outbreak of smallpox, in which the Vicar of Dean died of smallpox.

Curiosities.

Cappes.

Among many very curious records is this :—

1576, Pd for the discharge of the parish for not wearing of Cappes.—vs.

To help the Cap Trade in 1570 a Statute was passed which ordered every male person over six years old to wear a woollen cappe, on sondaies & holy daies. The penalty for each transgression was 3/4. Dean was fined 5/- for its transgression.

The Parish Herse.

Another curious record which occurs several times :—

1575. For nelles to mend the herse with.—ijd.

1714. Pd for a black herse cloth.—£1 12s. 6d.

1770. Pd for cleaning the black clothe. - 1s. 0d.

The herse was not a funeral car, but a frame which was placed over the shrouded body when it was brough to the church for burial, before coffins were in common use. The herse was removed when the body was brought to the grave.

About 1720 Coffins began to be used, but they were expensive.

1723. Pd for a coffin.—9/-
1729. John Ellel for a coffin for him.—9/-
1569. Received towards the makynge of the Jurerolose.—iijs iiijd.
1576. Paid for a Creste. *i.e.* A ridge tile. The ridge tile on a gable was often surmounted with a family crest, hence the word is applied to the tile itself.
1569. Pd for bredd and drynke when the tree fylled down in the Wyllyke (village)—iiijd.

Evidently it had to be removed from the road.

Dean and Marley had many experiences of this in the terrible gales of the autumn of 1929.

Some Ancient Records of Sheepstor.

The vicarage of Sheepstor had not always a resident incumbent, a Mr. Smith was vicar of Sheepstor as well as Bickleigh, and divine service was held in Sheepstor only once in three weeks. In the book of Parish Expenses we find, 1809, for eight bottles of wine, £1 13s. 5d., 1812, for five bottles for the sacrament, and five for the minister £2 8s. od. After this the entry is not specified for wine, but as Mr. Smith's bill, £2 os. od., or £2 1s. 3d.: in 1824 his bill amounted up to £3 15s. 6d.

The tradition is that there was a stone seat about the space where is now the village cross, and that after service Mr. Smith came there and, sitting with the village elders, produced and drank the contents of these bottles. The story as now told is that they tippled whiskey, but it would appear from the entries in the parish book that it was wine they drank, and indeed at the time whiskey was hardly drank in England. The Holy Communion was celebrated four times in the year, but after a while was reduced to three times, and in 1835 only once.

The Sheepstor people insist on it that it was here that the incident occurred (which has been told of other churches with a non-resident vicar, and only occasional services) that the vicar was prevented from entering the pulpit by his clerk, being told that " th' ould guse had bin a' settin' a brude there all the week, and 'twere a cruel shame to disturb her."

Some of the entries in the Parish Account Book are amusing – the spelling is extraordinary—1728, for the Dane Ruler, expenses 4d., 1733, spent when Dan ruler came to voisitt, 1/·, 1742, for a bottle of wine when the Dean Ruler came to visit, 3/-; and this seems to have been what henceforth the Rural Dean expected.

There are repeated entries of payments for the killing of foxes, badgers, otters.

1719, for killing a young fixen and a young fox,				6s.	8d.
1723, ,,	,,	8 fitches and a hedgehog,	-	1s.	3d.
1750, ,,	,,	an orter,	-	2s.	6d.
1762, ,,	,,	4 foxes,	-	£1 0s.	0d.
		4 oater and 1 bager	-	3s.	0d.

There was money given to wandering visitors in distress, but never largely.

1729, given to 2 sealors that logs (lost) teir (their) ship,	2s. 0d.
1732, Too 2 sealors that mad thear escape from Turkey with 28 men,	2s. 6d.
1738, to a man that has his tounge cut out of his mouth,	2s. 0d.

We have had some specimens of Sheepstor spelling, here are some more :—

1734, pd. for carigg of Lien	3s. 2d.
1735, pd. for a skittile tnat the prish was oner	2s. 0d.

The book containing distressments for the poor contains as well some curious matter. At one time the great drag on the parish funds was one Cherry, for whose breast the parish provided figs periodically.

CHAPTER XV.

The Poet's Corner.

THAT the wrestling was attended with danger to life or limb cannot be doubted. At Mary Tavy, in the churchyard, is the tombstone of John Hawkins, blacksmith, 1721 :—

> Here buried were some years before,
> His two wives and five children more :
> One Thomas named, whose fate was such
> To lose his life by wrestling much.
> Which may a warning be to all
> How they into such pastimes fall.

LITTLE JAN.

There is a Cornish ballad of a wrestling match between Will Trefry and " Little Jan ":—

> I sing of champions bold
> That wrestled, not for gold,
>   And all the cry was Will Trefry !
> That he should win the day.
> So Will Trefry, Huzzah !
> The ladies clap their hands and cry
>   Trefry ! Trefry ! Huzzah
>
> Then up sprang Little Jan,
> A lad scarce grown a man,
>   He said, Trefry ! I wot I'll try
> A hitch with thee this day.
> So little Jan, Huzzah !
> The ladies clap their hands and cry
>   O little Jan, Huzzah !
>
> They wrestled on the ground,
> His match Trefry had found,
>   And back he bore, in struggle sore,
> He felt his force give way ;
> So little Jan ! Huzzah !
> So some did say – but others nay.
>   Trefry, Trefry ! Huzzah !
>
> Then with a desperate toss
> Will showed the flying hoss.
>   And little Jan fell on the tan,
> And never more he spoke.
> O little Jan ! alack !
> The ladies say ; O woe's the day,
>   O little Jan—alack !

The Elfords had a mansion at Yelverton, which is actually Elford's Town. The earliest Elford of whom anything is known was John Elford who lived during the fifteenth century and whose son, also John, was buried at Sheepstor in 1517. They were a sporting family, and a ballad has been preserved relative to a doe from their park :

THE SILLY DOE.

Give ear unto my mournful song,
    Gay huntsmen every one,
And unto you I will relate
      My sad and doleful moan.
O here I be a silly Doe,
    From Elford Park I strayed,
In leaving of my company
      Myself to death betrayed.

The master said I must be slain
    For 'scaping from his bounds :
" O keeper, wind the hunting horn,
    And chase him with your hounds."
A Duke of royal blood was there,
    And hounds of noble race ;
They gathered in a rout next day,
    And after me gave chase.

They roused me up one winter morn,
    The frost it cut my feet,
My red, red blood came trickling down,
    And made the scent lie sweet.
For many a mile they did me run,
    Before the sun went down,
Then I was brought to give a fun,
    And fall upon the groun'.

The first rode up, it was the Duke ;
    Said he, " I'll have my will ! "
A blade from out his belt he drew
    My sweet red blood to spill.
So with good cheer they murdered me,
    As I lay on the ground ;
My harmless life it bled away,
    Brave huntsmen cheering round.*

*The ballad with its delightful air is given in the Garland of Country
    Song. Methuen & Co, London.

SHAVERCOMBE.

Where the Shavercombe wends
  A way to the Plym,
And never ends
  Its murmured hymn,
Is a dainty glen,
  Like a gem encased
By the dreary fen
  And the moorland waste.

Atop of the dell
  A waterfall
Like a silver bell
  To the moor doth call,
And drops sweet foam
  On a pool, steel-blue
    Where the ripples roam,
  Smiling at you.

Where the mountain ash
  Is the only tree
Bright with the splash
  Of the Shavercombe's glee;
And the milkwort mild
  Is the only flower
    And the only child
  Of this secret bower.   G.M.P.

One notion anciently held on the moor, was that the souls of unbaptised babes that had died passed wailing in the wind.

The wind blows cold on waste and wold,
  It bloweth night and day ;
The souls go by 'twixt earth and sky,
  Impatient, cannot stay.
They fly in clouds and flap their shrouds,
  When full the moon doth sail,
In dead of night, when lacketh light,
  We hear them pipe and wail.

And many a soul with des'late howl,
  Doth rattle at the door,
Or rove and rout, with dance and shout,
  Around the granite tor.
We hear a soul 'i th' chimney growl,
  That's drenched with the rain,
To wring the wet from winding sheet,
  And see the fire 'l were fain.

Bullaven Farm Hotel,

Harford, near Ivybridge, S. Devon.

TELEPHONE IVYBRIDGE 40Y2.

Situated actually on the moor, but with every comfort.

ELECTRIC LIGHT.   CENTRAL HEATING.

SEPARATE TABLES.   30 BEDROOMS.

TENNIS COURTS.

PRIVATE 9 HOLE GOLF COURSE.

:   :   SWIMMING POOL.   :

HUNTERS, HACKS and CHILDREN'S PONIES.
(instruction given).

Inclusive Terms from 3½ Guineas.

APPLY SECRETARY.

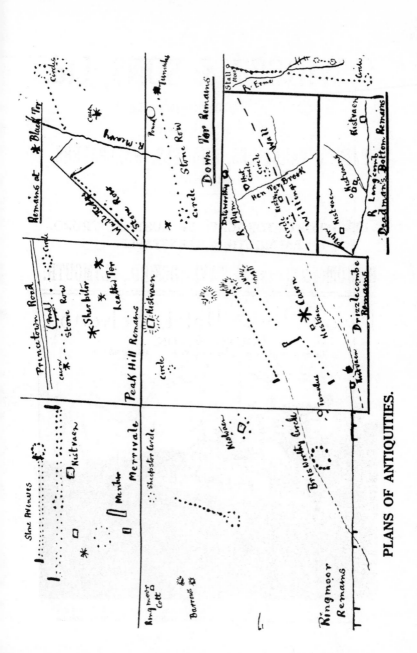

PLANS OF ANTIQUITIES.

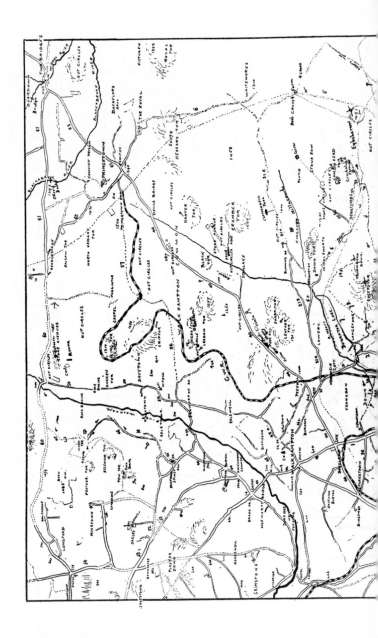

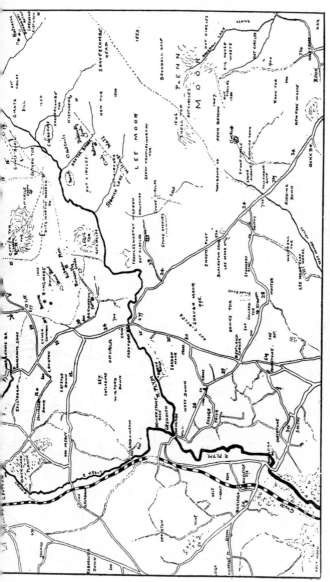

MAP OF THE S.W. QUARTER.

NOTES.

NOTES.

NOTES.

YELVERTON

FOR

FURNISHED AND UNFURNISHED HOUSES TO LET.
CHOICE BUILDING SITES.
PROPERTIES FOR SALE.

H. KITTO, F.A.L.P.A.,

HOUSE AGENT,

YELVERTON, S. DEVON.

Send three-halfpenny stamp for Illustrated Brochure.

Established 1828.

PIANOS

BECHSTEIN
HOPKINSON
MORLAND
ROGERS
SQUIRE LONGSON
STECK
STEINWAY

TURNER & PHILLIPS, L^{TD.}

MIDDLE OF GEORGE STREET

PLYMOUTH.

The Piano Specialists.

Appendices

APPENDIX I

BOOKS WRITTEN AND PUBLISHED BY THE REVEREND H. HUGH BRETON, M.A.

THE BEAUTIFUL DARTMOOR SERIES
(Originally called THE SHEEPSTOR SERIES):

1911   *Part 1:   Sheepstor and Its Border Lands.
1912   *Part 2:   The Northern Quarter of the Moor.
1913   *Part 3:   The Southern Quarter of the Moor.
1912   Part 4:   The Breezy Cornish Moors.
1912   Part 5:   Lands End and The Lizard.

(Parts 1 to 3 were also entitled Beautiful Dartmoor and Its Interesting Antiquities.)

THE MORWENSTOW SERIES OF SHILLING BOOKS:

1926   No. 1:   Morwenstow.
1926   No. 2:   The North Coast of Cornwall.
1926   No. 3:   Hawker of Morwenstow.
1926   No. 4:   The Heart of Dartmoor.

1928   The Great Blizzard of Christmas, 1927.
1929   *Spiritual Lessons from Dartmoor Forest
      (Part 1. "White Heather" and other studies)
      The Word Pictures of The Bible
      (New Testament, Part 1 "Some Aspects of Life").
1930   The Great Winter of 1928–29
      *Spiritual Lessons from Dartmoor Forest
      (Part 2. "Crystal Streams" and other studies)
      The Word Pictures of The Bible
      (New Testament, Part 2 "Personal Religion")
1931   *The Forest of Dartmoor (Part 1—South-East).
1932   *The Forest of Dartmoor (Part 2—South-West).

*Republished in facsimile edition 1990.

APPENDIX II

PROJECTED BOOKS BY THE REVEREND H. HUGH BRETON, M.A. NOT PUBLISHED

The Forest of Dartmoor (Part 3: North-West).
The Forest of Dartmoor (Part 4: North-East).

THE SPIRITUAL LESSONS FROM NATURE SERIES:

No. 1: Spiritual Lessons from Dartmoor Forest:
Part 3: Granite Chips in a Granite Country.
(Parts 1 and 2 were "White Heather" and "Crystal Streams" as listed in Appendix I)
No. 2: Spiritual Lessons from the Cornish Sea.
No. 3: Spiritual Lessons from the Cornish Mountains.

THE WORD PICTURES OF THE BIBLE:

New Testament, Part 3: "Life after Death".
Part 4: "Our Daily Life in God's Presence".
Part 5: "Some Picturesque Scenes in the New Testament".
Part 6: "Some Lessons from Bird and Animal Life in the New Testament".

Robert Furze, Gentleman

APPENDIX III

BOOKS WRITTEN BY MIKE LANG

Grand Prix!   Volume 1—1950 to 1965
Grand Prix!   Volume 2—1966 to 1973
Grand Prix!   Volume 3—1974 to 1980
Grand Prix!   The Grand Prix! Trilogy—1950 to 1980
*Grand Prix!   Volume 4—1981 to 1984

(Each sub-titled Race-by-Race account of Formula 1 World Championship motor racing and published by Haynes Publishing Group PLC, Sparkford, Nr Yeovil, Somerset BA22 7JJ).

*Due to be published shortly.